SING

VOLUME ONE

MARY SETRAKIAN

SING
FIND YOUR TRUE VOICE

Foreword by Sierra Boggess

Illustrations by Christopher Gunn

SUBBY PUBLISHING
New York, New York, USA

Library of Congress Control Number: 2022917125
Paperback ISBN: 979-8-9869557-0-4

Library of Congress Control Number: 2023900089
Hardcopy ISBN: 979-8-9869557-1-1

E-book ISBN: 979-8-9869557-2-8

First Edition
Printed in the United States of America
For more information visit www.marysetrakian.com

Cover design: Derek Bishop
Photography: David Noles
Illustrations: Christopher Gunn
Illustration of the referee: Emilie Autumn
Music notation graphics: Eloïse Mueller
Editor: Bud Kroll
Book design: Lissa Auciello-Brogan
Proofreader: Cheryl Lenser
Indexer: Cheryl Lenser

To my father,
Robert Setrakian

TABLE OF CONTENTS

VOLUME ONE

FOREWORD

By Sierra Boggess

Singing is the most joyous art form in the world. The freeing feeling of creating music with the sound that comes from within, the sound that is unique to each one of us, can truly heal and change the singer and the listener.

But singing can also be incredibly terrifying. When we sing we are being asked to expose something of ourselves – to tell stories using only our voice, to trust the notes as they leave our bodies and reach the ears of our audience. Because singing is so vulnerable, we often need someone alongside us that truly understands, who is trustworthy, who has our back, who is knowledgeable and knows how to guide us. For me, that person is Mary Setrakian.

I met Mary when I was just seventeen years old. She was teaching at a two week Musical Theatre Intensive in Breckenridge Colorado. I was a high school student obsessed with musical theatre, equally terrified and confident, and struggling with self-doubt and my worthiness. I had no idea just how much my world would be changed upon meeting her.

I clearly remember the first time I saw Mary work with a student in one of her master-classes. I had never seen someone ooze so much passion and genuine excitement for a student's progress. She was compassionate and real and empathetic and funny and so disinterested in anything false. She dared you to go to the depths, to delve into your vulnerability. Mary drew honest emotional performances out of people who were only accustomed to merely singing notes on a page. I quickly understood we shouldn't be looking for perfection in our vocal performance, we should be looking for truth. This is what I had been missing. No one had ever made me think about singing like this. I started to crave the process. I was hooked.

While working with Mary, I fell in love with singing through storytelling. I now know how to tell that story by dedicating each note to someone, by always knowing to *whom* I am singing, and *why* they need to hear it. It's a way of working that is so 'from the soul' that it's almost as if Mary is guiding you to remember who you really are. With Mary, no note is ever wasted. Vocal warmups aren't just something to get through. They all are endowed with meaning. "Do you have who you're singing to?" "What are you aware of?" "Drop in now," are just a few of the phrases she asks you to crystalize before even singing a scale. You always start from the place of knowing that your experiences have made you who you are as a human, so why not use them to sing as well?

The truth and the technique in Mary's method go hand in hand. I remember one particular masterclass when Mary was trying to get us to stop our over-the-top false acting beats and the unnecessary hand gestures in our songs. Mary casually blurted out the phrase "you are enough, you are so enough, it's unbelievable how enough you are." It stopped me in my tracks. I thought that was the most brilliant and hilarious phrase I had ever heard. It was almost as if she was pleading with us to trust ourselves before adding anything else. And really, if we don't know we are "enough," how else are we supposed to be raw and vulnerable as singers? How can the audience see themselves through us if we are apologizing for who we are in the process? In the same class, Mary taught us that the word "intimacy" means "into me, see." As performers, as singers, as actors, we are asking people to see us and see themselves through us. With this knowing as our foundation, we can then start building as performers and working in an authentic way.

I've worked with Mary for years. She has been by my side as teacher, cheerleader, and friend for each moment of my career. Her technique saved me when I was making my Broadway debut as Ariel in *The Little Mermaid* and later when I was portraying an opera singer in the Broadway revival of *Master Class*. When I was nervous having to sing both coloratura and rock belt in the Broadway production of *School of Rock*, Mary was there for me on every lunch break to remind me to focus on the breath and *The Revolutionary Send*. Mary is my first call for every Broadway audition, callback, and rehearsal process. Her methods are invaluable to anyone who has ever worked with her. Her technique is essential for every performer.

It excites me that with this book, you are now going to get to discover what Mary Setrakian has been teaching for decades. I know whether you are just starting out or have been singing for your entire life, this book is going to awaken something in you. I believe, just as Mary does, that we are all capable of singing, we just have to start somewhere.

So why not try? After all...you are enough!

PROLOGUE

First, a little story

Several times a year in New York City I teach a singing class. Anyone can come. The walls of the room where I hold the session are painted black. It's called a black box theater, which means no distractions – just the work. There are a few tiered benches, a piano, a blackboard, a high stool, and me.

Who, you might ask, comes to these classes? To my delight, there is always a diverse bunch. There are those who have sung on Broadway (still wanting to hone their craft), as well as trained dancers and actors who would like to add singing to their professional resumés. But this class doesn't just attract the pros. You see, singing can be a secret desire for many of us. I am often surprised by who else shows up.

Among the attendees has been a soccer mom who'd love to join her church choir but was too scared to audition. Also, a young professional guy, who wanted to stop being embarrassed at karaoke night singing off-key with his co-workers. I've had a top executive from Warner Brothers show up because her job requires a lot of public speaking. She felt that if she improved her singing voice, her speaking voice would improve too. (It did.) A high-profile banker took a "long lunch" to come to my class. He shared with me that when he was growing up, his parents convinced him that he'd never make it in showbusiness. How sad – it's what he truly loved. But happily, he had just landed the role of "King Arthur" in *Camelot* at his community theatre – and now he wanted my help. There were some adorable high school girls with stars in their eyes who dreamt of playing Christine in *Phantom of the Opera*, and others who said they "sing in the shower," but now hoped to find the courage to sing in public. There were even those who said they can't stand the sound of their own speaking voice. My adage is *"singing is born out of speaking,"* so getting their healthy, beautiful speech in place is a priority.

As the students line up, I can tell they are a bit nervous and apprehensive – perhaps realizing that, at a singing class, they'll actually have to sing. To assure them they have nothing to fear, I greet each person at the door. I ask about their singing experience and why they came.

But to tell you the truth, my "meet & greet" has an ulterior motive. I am secretly diagnosing their voices. I am checking into the essence of each person to find out: Is his voice free? Does she have emotional blocks? Does she think she's enough? Are they ready to share their vulnerability?

Singing, as I had to come to find out for myself, is not just about hitting the right notes. Don't get me wrong, that's important. I spent two years at the New England Conservatory because I wasn't confident in my high notes. Without the right technical information, high notes are hard! But even harder was coming to terms with the fact that singing is more than hitting perfect notes. A real voice, no matter what your vocal gift or range, must be shared from an emotional truth. Put more simply, if you are not connected to your emotions, your voice will lack that magical something that makes others stop and listen.

The first thing I do is *look*. I look to see how they are breathing. I look at their upper chest — is it heaving high? Inhaling at the top of the lungs with the chest rising up near the clavicles is *not* a healthy breath. In fact, it gives me a warning sign: *They are breathing above their true emotions. They are avoiding their painful feelings.* I call it the Panic Breath.

The most extreme case of the Panic Breath I ever saw was in a young actress who greeted me with so much enthusiasm that I couldn't wait to hear more about her. "Hi! I'm Nina!" she squealed, sounding just like Minnie Mouse. "So, tell me," I said, trying not to reveal the fact that I could clearly see her chest heaving high with every breath, "how do you want your voice to change?" To my shock, right there, with a line of people behind her, she said, "I'm here because, when I was a little girl, my mother was always trying to commit suicide. I know there is something wrong with my breathing and my voice. Can you help me?" I knew that I could. But I also knew that there would be tears and pain in class to heal her high-stakes vocal trauma.

Then, I look at their belly — is it held super tight? Or, is it moving easily with their breath? You see, to inhale naturally, the belly needs to release. (That's a discussion for later about how the famous diaphragm works.) I often spot an extra tight belly in athletes, from ballerinas to gym fanatics. Both models and military men are taught to hold the stomach *in*. But regular civilians are not immune either. Many of us pull our tummies in tight in order not to look fat. It's a noble idea, but it's not healthy for singing — or for life. The warning sign here is *holding it together*. If you are holding everything tight, there is no way to truly share your vulnerability — or your true voice.

And finally, I look at their shoulders — are they released, or are they lifting them up, as if to be holding the burdens of the world upon them?

Next, I *listen*. I listen for the timbre of the person's voice. Timbre is the sound – the texture – the character or quality of the voice. For example, is the timbre of their speaking voice high and airy, like Michael Jackson? Or, is the timbre rich, deep, and radiant, like James Earl Jones? Is their voice breathy and light, like Marilyn Monroe? Or, maybe they have the most annoying nasal sound, like "Janice" on the TV show *Friends*.

Or, worst of all, I hear a throaty timbre – those who speak right on the vocal cords, known as "vocal fry." This is more common than you would imagine among teenagers and millennials. These kids, who are full of unexpressed emotions, push their voices down. Creating that "bacon sizzling" sound in the throat, gives them a way to unknowingly cover their vulnerable feelings. Now they think they sound cool and relaxed. Distorting their true voices gives them a false courage that nothing can bother them, as if they are immune from the hurts of the world. On the contrary, they are unconsciously covering their emotions, and keeping their painful feelings at bay. Sadly, it's all an act, and one with very bad consequences.

Timbre exists because of vibration. I call this vibration Resonance. It's my job to make sure that each voice is *vibrating* and *resonating* in the most liberated way possible, without stress, blocks, or impediments.

As you sit there reading this, think of vibrating your voice around your mouth. Say "Hmmmmm." Do you feel a tickling vibration on your lips? Maybe your cheeks too? If not, relax your jaw, your tongue, and your lips a little bit more, and try again to really *feel* the buzzing sensation – "Hmmmmm." That vibration you feel around your mouth and cheeks is the healthy resonance I'm talking about.

Jamming the healthy resonance of the voice is not always the result of psychological issues (like vocal fry can be). It can occur, sadly, due to bad technical singing advice – of which there is plenty. Time and again, I hear a new student with a dissipated and airy sound. When I ask if their teacher told them to "open the throat" while singing, they say, "Yes, it's to get more resonance in my voice." Unfortunately, a throat that is open *too* wide minimizes the tone. Another side effect – the singer becomes vocally exhausted going through just one song! After we adjust the "open throat" dissipation, they not only discover their own beautiful, vibrant voice, but they can sing for hours without fatigue.

Next, after listening to the voice, I *feel*. I empathetically feel where the vibration of the resonance is living in the body of each student, and I feel how it is affecting them. How do I do this? In every note there are *overtones* – extra tones, also called *frequencies,* that we can't hear with our naked ear. A voice vibrating properly will generate these overtones which are stacked on top of the fundamental tone (the note we do hear) like a skyscraper: There's the fundamental frequency in the basement, and then the overtones ring on the lower floors, medium floors, and high above in the penthouse. Through a kind of osmosis, I diagnose each voice to see if these overtones are ringing freely. If not, how are they physically and emotionally being jammed?

There are those who are speaking way too high, above their true voice — a soft, airy, floaty sound that has no grounding. This can be a way for them to disconnect from their sexuality and painful emotions. Michael Jackson was a severe case. It's well known that he was abused by his father at a very young age. I believe that, in desperately trying to escape from his pain, Michael Jackson stayed a little boy — like Peter Pan who never grew up — speaking above his true voice in a high, disconnected tone.

I've also witnessed talented African American men in my class who unconsciously suppress the full resonance and power of their voices by speaking softly. I make sure these talented men are aware they no longer have to soften their power. It deeply troubles me that this vocal issue reveals a truth about prejudice in a world where much of White society is frightened by strong, young Black males. In order not to come off as "scary," these good and compassionate men unconsciously soften the tone of their voices. In doing so, they diminish their resonance and vocal presence to accommodate others. This must stop. We need the full power of their voices in our world.

There are others who dampen the highest overtones in their voice by pushing their voice way down low. I feel that these people are scared that they will be "too much." They don't dare have high tones in their voice — maybe they'll take up too much space. I've seen a little sister who didn't want to surpass her big sister, so she spoke softly, like a mouse. I worked with a son who wanted his father to accept him, so he pushed his voice into his throat and sounded like a frog. Their voices were scratchy and unappealing. But it was a way to protect themselves from being in their greatness — God forbid if she was better than her sister, or if he stood up to his father. They were not aware, because it had become a way of life.

So, still at the door, I am assessing their problems. I ask each person individually, "What do you need today? In what ways do you want your voice to be better?" Their answers (or lack of answers) give me great insight into what I should focus on with them individually, and how those answers relate to my first *look, listen, and feel* assessment of them. Maybe there's a theme that day — maybe there's a large percentage of those who are speaking in their throat. Maybe most of them are diminishing their power, and they don't know it. Maybe I'll focus the whole class in a specific way.

After our "meet & greet," everyone takes their seat on the benches, waiting for their first instruction. You might think that, having had a chance to chat with me, everyone would be pretty relaxed. No way. I look out to a sea of legs crossed and arms folded in front of chests. This is a habit we all do for protection. Crossing the arms and legs is the perfect way to hide and protect yourself – like when you're riding the subway in New York City. But in singing class, we pray that all of our emotions are available to us – not guarded. So, first things first: I announce, "For the entire class, no one is allowed to sit with crossed arms or legs. Stay open!"

I turn on music. But we are not going to sing – not yet. We're going to move. I make every student come down the tier to the center in front of the class and yell their full name – first and last. One of the youngest students, a girl who is there with her mother, leans over (her mother later tells me) and says, "Get me out of here. I can't do that." This same young woman has gotten up on a stage multiple times to sing and dance, but the thought of shouting out her own name in a black box theatre terrifies her. But there will be no exceptions. After she yells her name, the students on the benches repeat her name exactly how she yelled it. Then, she must do a dance move – any dance move she likes. The rest of the class must drop into her character and move their bodies exactly as she has done. Why do I do this? Because it is powerful to say your name. We don't say our full name very often, and we certainly never shout it. It's even more empowering to hear a whole group repeat your name. And for me, the teacher? It's revealing to see if she is brave enough to shout her full name. Will she be brave enough to sing?

As for the dancing, I am asking each person to take an even bigger risk: to move in their own truth – whatever that truth might be – in front of others. I am asking the rest of the class to reproduce that movement because this requires them to step outside of themselves, and, just maybe, move as someone they never thought they could be.

Now it is time for each person to get up and sing individually for me. What, you might ask, do people actually get up and sing? Everything – from opera to rock, from folk to Broadway. A few of them panic and don't know what to sing, so I tell them to sing "Happy Birthday." That's fine. As they sing for me, one by one, I'm gauging their courage. Can they take a risk and sing no matter what level they are at? Are they willing to sing out and share their emotions? I often compliment their efforts: "That was fucking great!" (The students crack up.) My swearing is kind of a ruse – if I'm a little crass and crazy, they just might conjure up a little more courage to take a risk. I hope they take the bait.

By the end of the singing, there is a calm that comes over the room. Not one person has run out in tears – quite the contrary. A few are actually smiling! They are beginning to talk to each other. The young girl who didn't want to shout her name now can't stop talking: "Gosh, I feel so much better!" I tell her that I have trained Hollywood stars who say the same thing after a singing lesson (like the late James Gandolfini who I'll talk about later).

It's time to turn to the blackboard to teach the techniques that I learned from my truly gifted master teachers. I pause and reflect for just a moment. It always stuns me to realize how I stand on the shoulders of so many, who gave me the knowledge that I have spun into my own method – from my public high school's music department with vocal masters JD Nichols and Gary B. Walker, to my private voice teachers throughout my youth beginning with Corinne Swall and Marie Gibson, then Mark Pearson, Phyllis Curtain, and Joan Heller – to my acting mentor of thirty years, Susan Batson. My career and my life would not be so full without their guidance. I do indeed stand on their shoulders as I step to the blackboard. Maybe someday, in the near or far future, you too will take the information you've learned from others and in this book and integrate it into your own method. I'd be honored to have you stand on my shoulders. May we all keep passing it forward.

The blackboard is waiting. We are off and running, studying the voice techniques that connect to our emotions – learning on our feet how to release our demons, our pain, our personal stories, and lift it all to the art, joy, and the magic of singing.

INTRODUCTION

SINGING IS A MIRACLE

It's your best friend's birthday, and it's time for that special moment. The cake with candles is being paraded out to the living room, and all the lights are turned off. You start singing that famous song: *Happy Birthday to you...*Without a thought, your voice goes to the exact melody of "Happy Birthday." We all join in. We all know "Happy Birthday." We all recognize the tune, and our voices follow your lead perfectly. Even if somebody waivers off pitch, we're singing the song together. Our voices are in the air. We have joined the birds in the God-given gift of song!

How did our brains and bodies and vocal cords know how to sing the exact melody of "Happy Birthday?" Let's face it — singing is a miracle.

Even with this miracle, there is much you can do to improve your singing voice. With this book, it is my passionate pleasure to help you discover your personal, one-of-a-kind singing voice, and bring it to its full potential. From the seasoned professional who is on a stage every day, to the amateur who sings in the shower, to those of you who believe that singing is beyond your reach — I think you can sing — *really* sing.

> **Anyone who is born with vocal cords has the capability to speak and sing. I believe the voice is a spiritual channel. It opens up a universe of communication, creativity, and intimacy through sound and vibration.**

THERE'S ONLY ONE YOU

Take a look in the mirror. That's YOU! There is no other like you. And just like fingerprints and snowflakes, there is no other voice like yours. We have seen judges on TV shows and know-it-alls around the world give their opinions on whose voice is the best, worst, or downright awful. I believe every individual has something special. There certainly are different kinds of vocal gifts that the Universe hands out, but who is to say what is the best gift?

Rex Harrison didn't want to accept the role of Professor Higgins in the original 1956 musical *My Fair Lady* because he said he couldn't sing at all. And yet, his songs in *My Fair Lady*, largely spoken, moved his audience so much that most people don't even remember that he rarely sang. He went on to win a Tony and Oscar for his stage and film performances. When the great dancer/singer Fred Astaire had his first audition, the feedback was "Can't sing. Can dance a little." True, his voice was light as a reed, but Fred Astaire's honesty and simple delivery made him one of the most sought-after singers by the leading composers of the 1930's, including Cole Porter, Irving Berlin, Johnny Mercer, and the Gershwin brothers. These talented composer-lyricists knew that their lyrics would be *heard and felt*. A slight figure who could *really* sing (and dance *a lot*), Fred Astaire became the number one recording artist of his day, introducing more standards from the Great American Songbook than any other singer. He lived his potential.

That is my dream for you – to live your potential.

WHY DO YOU LOVE TO SING?

Why do you love to sing in the shower, or sing into your hairbrush in your bedroom with the door shut tight, or sing in your car where nobody can hear you? It's cathartic, right? You feel your emotions, and you sing them out. Love! Anger! Loss! Joy! It's your own Private Idaho where nobody can judge you. Raising up your voice in your privacy, no matter how good or bad it sounds, brings you joy.

How about singing *in front* of people with all that truth, depth, and emotion? Did you just get nervous? Truly expressing oneself through song is a vulnerable journey. Exposing that intimacy can be downright frightening.

Many voice teachers will tell you that singing is all about voice technique. I've even heard some say not to let the emotions get in the way of singing and to focus only on technique. Of course, technique matters – a lot. But singing is not just about hitting technically perfect notes every time.

Singing begins with the fact that you are a living, breathing human being with feelings that need to be expressed. Singing in the shower, or in your room or car where nobody can hear you, allows you to connect to *your* truth. Your real emotions carry you through the song, revealing your fears, vulnerabilities, and secret desires, in a way that others can share. And when you do share your song with an audience, it becomes universal. Others can *feel* you, and release their fears, vulnerabilities, and secret desires just by listening to your song.

My method integrates it all, connecting voice technique *with* your emotions, and *how* to share your vulnerability in song, even publicly. Believe it or not, the technical side actually helps the emotional side — and vice-versa.

Remember these words:

> ***Your voice technique is in your emotions,***
> ***and your emotions are in your voice technique***

THE SINGING CONNECTION

Old School Voice Technique

The traditional voice teacher is interested in helping you make a beautiful *sound* with your voice by focusing on voice technique. Yes, voice technique is extremely important, but this is putting the singer in a little box just focusing on BODY and MIND.

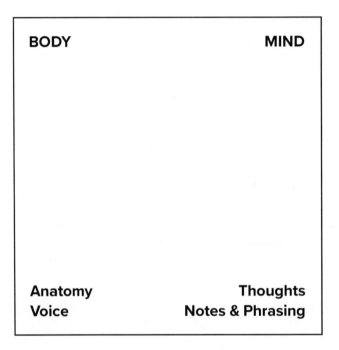

BODY

MIND

Anatomy
Voice

Thoughts
Notes & Phrasing

- Learn how your **Body** works – Voice Technique
- Use your **Mind** – how to read music – how to do musical phrasing – how to make dynamics like *crescendo* and *diminuendo*

How about deeply moving an audience, and at the same time, discovering your personal one-of-a-kind tone? The combination of connecting voice technique *with* your emotions is the secret of reaching one's true vocal potential.

Now we add one more element to the Old School Voice Technique: **Emotions**

BODY – MIND – EMOTIONS

YOU are the VESSEL. This is the process of how to find your true voice:

- Learn how your **Body** works – Voice Technique
- Use your **Mind** to understand all of the concepts
- Courageously step into your **Emotions**
- and SING
- SEND – and let your gift LIVE in the most powerful and dynamic way possible

Your Mind, Body, and Emotions

go through you

– THE VESSEL –

Body	Mind	Emotions
Voice	Intellect	Feelings
Voice Technique	Thoughts	Emotional Life
Physical Body	Imagination	Intimacy
Air	Cognition	Vulnerability
Vibration	Action	Sensation

and the result is magic.

I call it

THE REVOLUTIONARY SEND

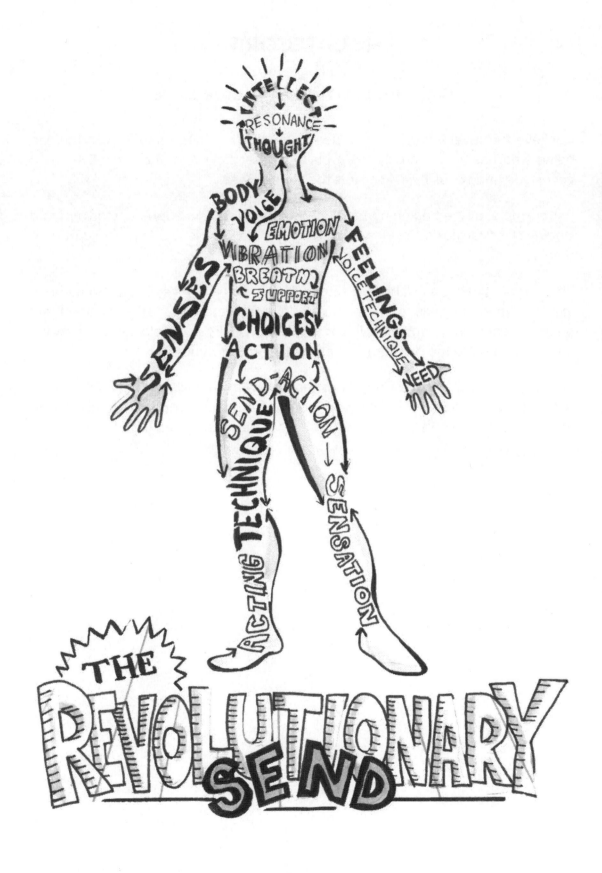

THE CATEGORIES

Who are you now? – Home Base

I believe that every singer (and when I say every singer, I mean *every* human being who has vocal cords), has a place where their voice naturally lives as a *vocal type* and *vocal style*. I call this the **Home Base**.

For example, at the beginning of my career I started as a soprano, studying and singing classical music. So, Mary Setrakian's Home Base is *The Classically Trained Singer*.

The following categories I have created will give you a glance at *your* Home Base (maybe you identify with more than one). In every category I list, you'll see that I diagnose each singer and explain certain needs, desires, and blocks, and how we are going to solve the problem of that particular prototype.

Please find yourself in The Categories that follow and jump to the ones that resonate with you. Use this as an outline of how you're going to organize yourself with the work ahead. Who are you now? And, where are you going from here?

THE CATEGORIES

The Classically Trained Singer

The Musical Theatre / Broadway Singer

The Pop / Rock / Jazz / R&B / Country Singer / Rapper

The Actor

The Dancer

The Conductor / Composer / Instrumentalist

You Sing In The Shower

You Think You're Tone Deaf

The Classically Trained Singer

If your Home Base is The Classically Trained Singer, *you may relate to one or more of the following:*

- You are a professional singer
- You hold a degree in Music/Voice
- You come from a musical family
- You sang as a child
- You've studied classical music with one or more voice teachers
- You want to be a professional singer

Problems you might have:

- You've studied a lot of singing technique, but it doesn't always work for you
- You feel technically proficient, but you'd like to connect to the material better
- You're always worried if you sound good enough
- You're not in touch with all of your needs and emotions – Your career and personal life aren't going where you want them to go

Let's solve the problems:

- We will look at the singing technique together in the quest to *really* understand it – With this clarity, the singing becomes effortless because it's exactly how your body works and what your body wants
- We will take the journey to connect your emotional life with your voice technique so that they work seamlessly together: Your voice technique is in your emotions – Your emotions are in your voice technique – If you just focus on voice technique, you're not attaining the most beautiful sound you can make
- We'll add the emotional tools of using your past, your imagination, and your true feelings for your artist
- Opening your emotions and singing through them will open every aspect of your being – helping your career and personal life blossom

The Musical Theatre / Broadway Singer

If your Home Base is The Musical Theatre / Broadway Singer, *you may relate to one or more of the following:*

- You work in musicals
- You hold a degree in Theatre, and/or are studying to sing, act, and dance
- You come from a musical family
- You were always putting on shows as a child
- Your dream is to be on Broadway

Problems you might have:

- You have a really great voice, but you aren't getting the jobs you want
- You know you have acting talent, but aren't sure how to apply that talent to your singing
- As a Broadway Singer, you must sing eight shows a week – you need more stamina

Let's solve the problems:

- We will connect your acting talent *with* your voice, identifying and applying the acting tools that will take your work to the next level in both auditions, and on the stage
- We will look at the singing technique together to make sure you're singing with great vocal ease and vocal health, even with a schedule of eight shows a week
- Your gifts as a performer will reveal themselves as you become aware of the special qualities that only you have – You are enough

The Pop / Rock / Jazz / R&B / Country Singer / Rapper

If your Home Base is The Pop / Rock / Jazz / R&B / Country Singer / Rapper, *you may relate to one or more of the following:*

- You have a band
- You have a degree in Music

- You've been singing since you were a child

- Artists you admire influence your work

- You eat, breathe, and live music

Problems you may have:

- You often get vocally tired and/or lose your voice

- You can hear that you're off pitch sometimes, but you don't know how to fix it

- You love singing and have an extensive repertoire, but you want to have a deeper connection with your songs

- You think that you're really good, but you'd like a bigger fan base

Let's solve the problems:

- Some voice teachers believe that singing classical music is the only way to have a good voice technique and sing properly – They say that if you sing in other styles you'll hurt your voice – I come from a classical technique, but have found a profound way to connect those tools to every style – My technique will prove that you can sing in any style you love with great vocal health and a deep connection

- Even if you've got a lot of energy, an amazing voice, and fantastic stage presence, there is something more – We will explore together how to connect your true self to your work – You'll have fans lining up around the block

The Actor

If your Home Base is The Actor, *you may relate to one or more of the following:*

- You're a professional actor

- You have a degree in Acting

- You have studied acting with one or more teachers

- You call yourself an actor

Problems you might have:

- You love to sing and want to do it more

- You know you can sing, but it intimidates you

- You know you're a terrible singer, but you want to do it anyway

- You're scared to death of singing

- You have low self-confidence sometimes

Let's solve the problems:

- Because you're an actor, you're already ahead of the game — You have something very special to bring to singing: your acting technique

- With my voice technique we are going to connect the hard work you've already done as an actor *with* your singing

- Singing starts from talking, and, as an actor, you already know how to talk — And the singing technique will help the acting

- You will have more self-confidence — Let's open more doors in your life

The Dancer

If your Home Base is The Dancer, *you may relate to one or more of the following:*

- You're a professional dancer

- You have a degree in Dance

- You love musical theatre

- You were always dancing around the house as a child

- You have worked as a dancer, or been a part of many school musicals and/or dance troupes

- You want to work professionally in musical theatre or as a pop star

Problems you might have:

- You can sing, but you'd like your voice to be stronger

- It's hard to sing while you're dancing

- When you audition, you always worry if you sound good enough

- You get so nervous singing

- You don't feel that people hear you in your life — It's hard to make yourself clear

Let's solve the problems:

- Once you understand the voice technique, you can make it live side by side with your dancer

- You will now call yourself an actor – As a dancer, you're already an actor – Are you confident in certain styles of dance? What makes you so good? Do you trust that you are sexy? Athletic? Emotional when you dance? We will connect the acting elements you already have as a dancer with your voice

- In auditions you'll finally be able to focus on the real work whether the judges like you or not

- You will find the truth in your life that is missing – You'll be able to say what you mean

The Conductor / Composer / Instrumentalist

If your Home Base is The Conductor / Composer / Instrumentalist, *you may relate to one or more of the following:*

- You're a professional musician

- You have a degree or degrees in Music

- You're a highly trained musician

- You work with singers all of the time

- You have a fantastic ear, maybe even perfect pitch

- You've been studying music since you were a child

- You want to be a professional musician

Problems you might have:

- You can hear exactly what's wrong with the singers' voices, but when you tell them what is wrong, they aren't able to apply your notes

- You can't always get from your singers the emotional content of the material

- You like to sing, but you know you could sound better

- People think you are egotistical and full of yourself

Let's solve the problems:

- It's time for you to walk in your emotional life and connect it to voice technique – It will help your craft as a musician

- This technique connects the body, the mind, and the emotions – As a singer, your body is your instrument – All of your passion to create music will live in your body, and connect to your emotions – We will bring your work to a new level

- Because you are walking in the shoes of a singer connecting voice technique with the emotional life, you will understand firsthand how to talk to your singers for your projects

- You will understand *who you are* – Sharing your intimacy in your art will bring those in your life closer to you

You Sing In The Shower

If your Home Base is You Sing in the Shower, *you may relate to one or more of the following:*

- You secretly would love to sing in public

- You're in a chorus or would love to join one

- Your friends think you have a great voice

- You love to sing

Problems you might have:

- A family member told you that you can't make a living singing – like your mom saying, "That's nice honey, but when are you going to get a real job?"

- You constantly compare yourself to other singers

- You have trouble communicating

- You aren't always happy in your job and you feel stuck in your life

Let's solve the problems:

- If you sing in the shower and you picked up this book, maybe you want to take your singing more seriously – If so, let's go

- Enough of talking about singing – It's time to SING – You did it, you're doing it, it's done

- Singing is a channel of communication – Because you're giving yourself the permission to SING, you'll be able to communicate better in all areas of your life

You Think You're Tone Deaf

If You Think You're Tone Deaf *and don't have a Home Base, you may relate to one or more of the following:*

- You secretly would love to sing

- Listening to music is a huge part of your life

- When no one is listening, like when you are alone in your car, you sing at the top of your lungs

Problems you might have:

- A family member, friend, or teacher told you *not* to sing

- You've heard more than once that you have a terrible voice

- You can hear that you're off pitch, but you don't know how to fix it

- You feel stuck in your life, and are not able to say everything you need to say

Let's solve the problems:

- You think you are tone deaf? I don't – True, there are different levels of the gift of a good voice, but don't give up – You'll find that when you implement the two sides of my method – voice technique and the emotional life – you will be a singer

- When you free your voice with the right technique, and then tell a specific story that means something to you through song, the pitches will line up – The category of "tone deaf" disappears – It's a miracle

- You will speak and communicate better with your one-of-a-kind power

HOW THE BOOK WILL BE ORGANIZED

To take full command of your voice, you must take responsibility for your instrument – YOU. I'm here to share with you the tools that changed my life. I've organized these tools such a way that they are easy to follow.

In Part I, the first ten chapters, I will guide you through my method, *The Revolutionary Send,* as well as the "how to exercises." (All exercises are highlighted by a gray shaded background.) Alongside the descriptive content, you'll read many stories about the students I've worked with, from famous superstars to students from around the world. I've even included my personal stories of my journey in this work. We will make clear the Confusing Phrases we often hear when studying voice and bust some Myths about singing. In Part II, you'll find all the exercises in one place, so you'll have them available any time you need them. In addition, there's a Healing Exercise for your voice.

I suggest that you read the book straight through in order. Even if you've already studied a certain element, please don't skip a chapter or an exercise. You might find a tweak you never thought of, or an adjustment that helps you. And in any case, it's always good to practice! (I've taught these elements for decades now, and every time I teach them, I get to practice too.) Then, go back any time you want to focus on the sections that you personally need – whether it's to understand Support – sing high notes – connect your vulnerability to your singing – be inspired by a story – prepare a song, etc.

I want these pages to be a guide for you to find your true voice – to give you the tools and inspiration – for your career, your community, your life.

The
Revolutionary
Send

introduction

Welcome to *The Revolutionary Send*!

There are two sides to my method, *The Revolutionary Send*: The Voice Technique Side and the Emotional Life Side. Each side has five elements:

Five elements of Voice Technique

Five elements of the Emotional Life

We are going to walk through each of the ten elements over the course of this book and check off each one together as we go.

THE REVOLUTIONARY SEND

VOICE TECHNIQUE SIDE	EMOTIONAL LIFE SIDE
1. The Breath	1. Personalization
2. Support	2. Fourth Wall
3. Resonance	3. Sensory Condition
4. Floors	4. Need
5. Pyramid	5. Action

No matter who you are — a professional singer, a member of a choir, a lover of community theater, someone who can't sing "Happy Birthday" on pitch, or someone who just wants to improve your speaking voice, I start the first voice lesson the same way with every student. We begin with the first three elements on the **Voice Technique Side** of my method.

1. **THE BREATH**

2. **SUPPORT**

3. **RESONANCE**

> **These three elements are not only important for singing.**
> **They are the three essential tools for speaking with great vocal health.**
> **"Singing is born out of speaking."**

chapter one

THE BREATH

ELEVEN YEARS OLD AND SIX FEET TALL
Why do I feel like I'm going to die?

I had the great privilege of working with a talented youth group – about twenty tweens and teenagers from St. Maarten. They all came to New York City to study in a program called *Art Saves Lives*.

As the kids walked through the door, I could tell they were committed to sing with me that day, all happily scurrying to their seats. The youngest girl in the class was eleven years old, and *six feet tall*. She was darling, soft-spoken, and seemed just as eager to learn as the eighteen-year-old charming young adults.

I began the workshop as I always do, with the first element, The Breath (the inhale). Before beginning my analysis on how the lungs work, I immediately observed that the kids had one of the most common problems with The Breath: inhaling way high in the chest, up around the clavicles. I call it the Panic Breath. Fortunately, after my instruction, they were all able to change the high Panic Breath to the breath that the body uses naturally: breathing at the bottom of the lungs with the tummy releasing out and in (just the same as sleeping at night), which I call the Economical Breath.

Now, with their breath adjusted perfectly, I was ready to move onto the second element, Support. Suddenly, up shot the hand of the youngest girl.

"Mary..."

"Yes?"

"Why do I feel like I'm going to die?"

(Pause)

"Oh. You feel like you're going to die?"

"Yes," she said serenely.

"Well…," I collected my thoughts, "let's think about this together. You are eleven years old. Right?"

"Right."

"And you're quite tall for your age – six feet tall?"

"Right."

"And I can imagine that that's not easy. Is that true?"

"Yes."

"So, before we did the Economical Breath, you were breathing high at the top of your lungs. Right?"

"Yes."

"When we breathe at the top of the lungs in the Panic Breath, we are *avoiding* our real feelings. You see, the Economical Breath actually gets us in touch with our true emotions. You didn't want to feel any painful emotions, so you held your tummy tight and were breathing *above* your feelings, high in your chest. But now, by changing to the Economical Breath, you just discovered *exactly* how you feel: You walk around in life feeling like you are going to die."

"Oh," she said softly.

"The good news is that you are not going to die! You are breathing like your body wants to breathe, which is really healthy! You are safe here. And you are special exactly how you are – six feet tall! As you breathe naturally, your body is going to release the idea that you are dying and realize that you are safe. Hey, let's see what happens! We have four more hours in class today. Keep breathing in this healthy breath for the full four hours, and let's see how you feel at the end of class. Okay?"

"Yes! Okay!"

I checked in with this darling girl at the end of the class.

"So, how do you feel?"

"Wonderful!"

THE BREATH

1. Voice Technique Side

THE BREATH – Inhale

The Goal: To learn how the lungs in your body actually inflate. Then apply this natural breath to your own breathing patterns. I call it the Economical Breath.

Why This Is Important: Breathing too high in the chest, shallow breathing, and even periods of unconsciously holding your breath, are all signs of unresolved psychological stress and incorrect body patterns that can stand in your way when you start to sing.

What Has To Change: Your willingness to confront these issues that are preventing you from letting your body breathe naturally, the way it does when you fall asleep. For some of us, just seeing this pointed out may be enough. For others, confronting our demons may be necessary.

"How would you describe the perfect singer's breath – the inhale?"

That's the first question I ask every new student. I'm not trying to test the student. I'm only curious what they've been taught and/or what they've heard. The answers give me clues into what, if anything, is blocking their breath as they inhale.

 The following phrases are some of the answers I often hear. Some of the phrases are wrong, some of them could be right, but I find all of them to be confusing without further explanation:

CONFUSING PHRASES – THE BREATH:

1. "Breathe into your belly"
2. "Breathe into the diaphragm"
3. "Push your stomach out"
4. "Take a low, deep breath"
5. "Tank up as much air as possible"
6. "Breathe into your back"
7. "Tank up like a tire around your ribs"

We will go back to these *Confusing Phrases* at the end of the chapter and examine each one. But first, let's learn how to breathe:

LEARNING WHAT THE BODY ALREADY KNOWS
Just Breathe

We hear it all the time – *Just breathe*. Sounds simple, right? I mean, we must breathe to stay alive, and yet for some, to breathe "naturally" can be complicated because of stress and bad habits.

The body can learn bad habits that hinder the "natural" breath. Muscle memory is strong, so if wrong habits are in place, it may take time to change those old patterns. Correct practice makes for good muscle memory. Let's practice correctly from the beginning!

Our task is to *Learn what the body already knows*. Let's learn to inhale as we naturally do when we sleep at night. That is the Economical Breath we want to hone for speaking, singing, and life.

"Where are the lungs?"

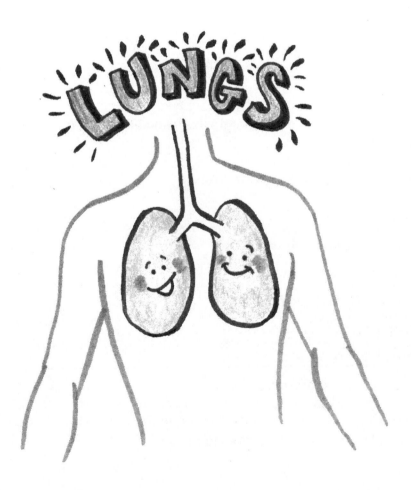

The lungs are located in the chest cavity. We must breathe into the actual lungs. Sounds easy, but sometimes we are led astray.

> *Have you ever taken a yoga or relaxation class where the teacher has said something like "breathe into your knee?" This may be very helpful for relaxation and health, but for singing, you must look at the body as your instrument. You are a singing athlete. You breathe into the lungs, and the lungs are not in your knee.*

"When you are sleeping at night not thinking about it, does the body inhale at the top of the lungs, or at the bottom of the lungs?"

If you said the *bottom of the lungs*, you're right! The bottom of the lungs is the area around the bottom of the ribcage. Think of starting your inhale there.

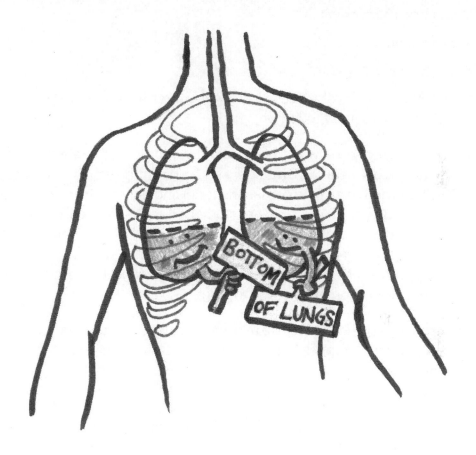

THE BREATH

Bella Thorne
Breathe into the Bottom of the Lungs

Seventeen-year-old Disney starlet Bella Thorne rushed into my studio. "Sorry I'm late. The paparazzi were following me." Bella seemed as flustered with the photographers as she was with the fact that she had to actually *sing* at her voice lesson.

"I understand you have a movie coming up – *Midnight Sun* – and you're playing a singer/songwriter?"

"Yes, but I don't like to sing."

"Interesting that you chose to do this movie then."

"Well, I don't sing on pitch."

"We'll fix that."

"And, I hate voice lessons."

"No problem, I hate voice teachers." Bella's eyes widened. "Let's get to work. We'll figure it out together."

We began as I always do – with The Breath. Everyone is different, but for Bella, her breath was super shallow, and she was holding her stomach as tight as a drum. Why? Bella had been a professional model and dancer since she was a little girl, so she was taught to always hold her stomach tight. In addition, being stressed out by the craziness that fame can bring – like the paparazzi running after her – she was literally *holding it together.* When I instructed Bella to release her tight tummy and to *let the air enter into the bottom of her lungs* just as her body does naturally, she looked happy and ready to sing.

Bella Thorne starred in her first movie musical, *Midnight Sun,* and sang with beauty, pathos, and perfectly on pitch – thanks to her newly found Economical Breath laying the groundwork.

Right before Bella flew off to Canada to record her songs for the movie, I had to ask her, "You said the first day we met that you *hate voice lessons*. Has something changed? Do you like voice lessons now?" She gathered her thoughts and said,

"You took the time to understand me – to connect with me – and you gave me something that I can actually use – like *how to breathe*. Yes, I like these voice lessons."

"How do the lungs inflate?"

The Famous Diaphragm

When it comes to breathing, we always hear about the diaphragm (so much, that I call it *famous*). **But *what is the diaphragm? Where is it? What does it do*?**

The diaphragm is an *involuntary muscle* shaped like a pancake that lives right under the lungs around the bottom of the ribcage.

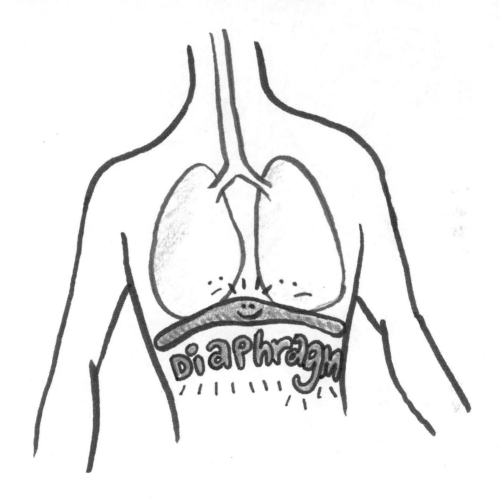

"The diaphragm is essential in the process of air getting into our lungs, but how does it work?"

Think of the lungs in your chest like two balloons. These two balloons must blow up for you to breathe, but they can't do it by themselves.

Here is a fact that we rarely hear about:

There is a nerve on each side of your neck called the PHRENIC NERVE.

The body says, ***I need air in my lungs!***

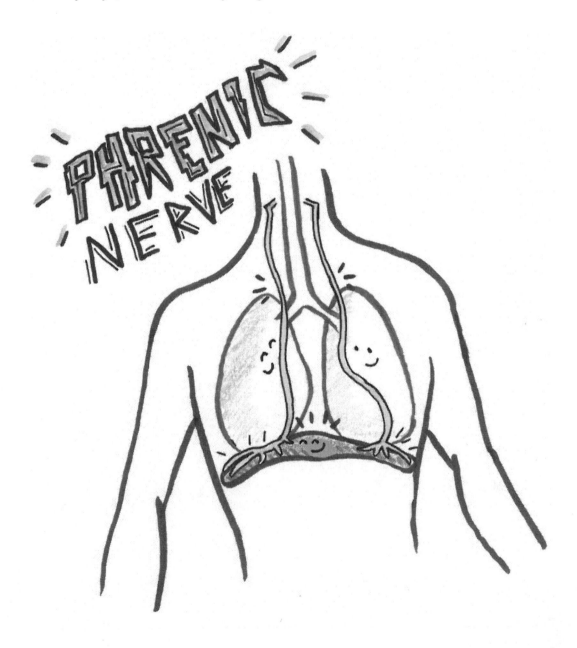

1. **The phrenic nerve** "hears" the request and **sends a signal to the diaphragm**.

The diaphragm receives the signal and responds, ***Got it, Boss!***

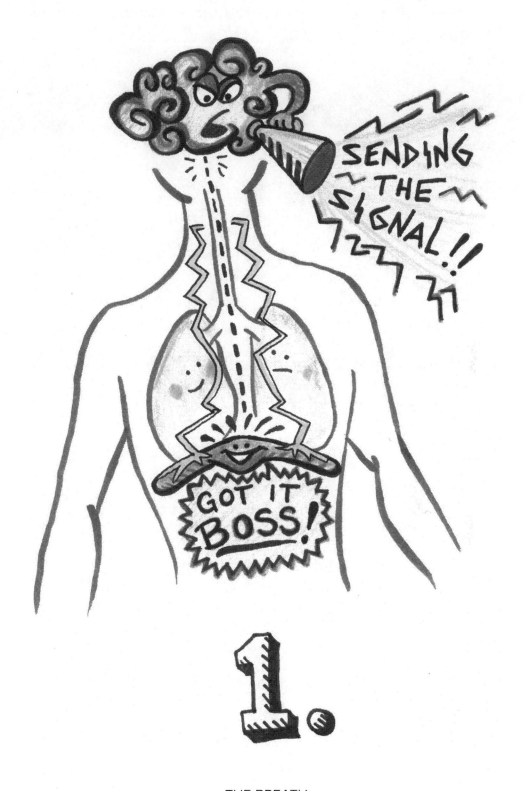

THE BREATH

2. Then the magic happens: **The diaphragm *contracts*.** This causes two things to happen: As it drops down into the abdominal cavity, the diaphragm pushes aside the organs, so your tummy naturally goes OUT. At the same time, it drops *down* pulling the lungs with it. This contraction **creates a *vacuum* in the lungs.**

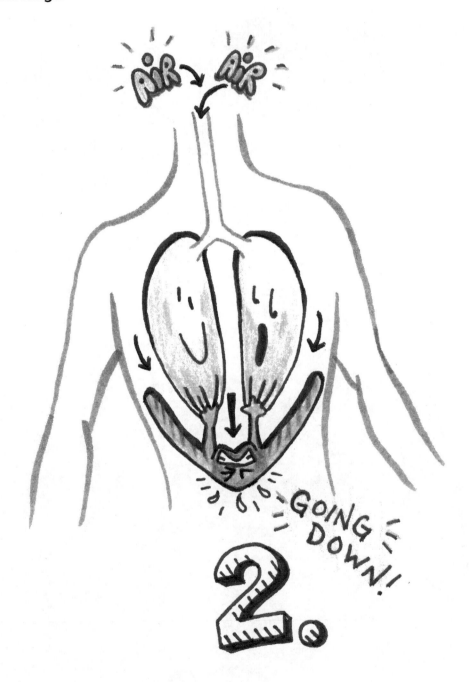

3. Because of the vacuum, air rushes into the lungs. **That's The Breath!**

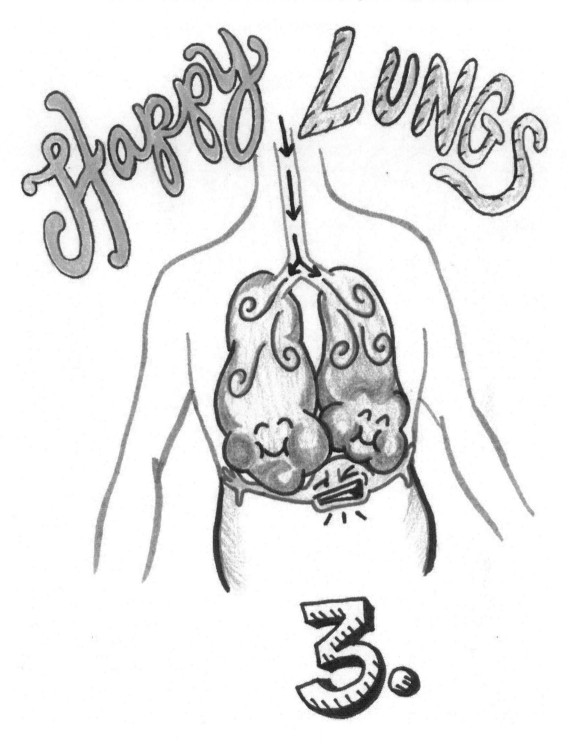

HOW TO TAKE AN ECONOMICAL BREATH

All Illustrations in Order

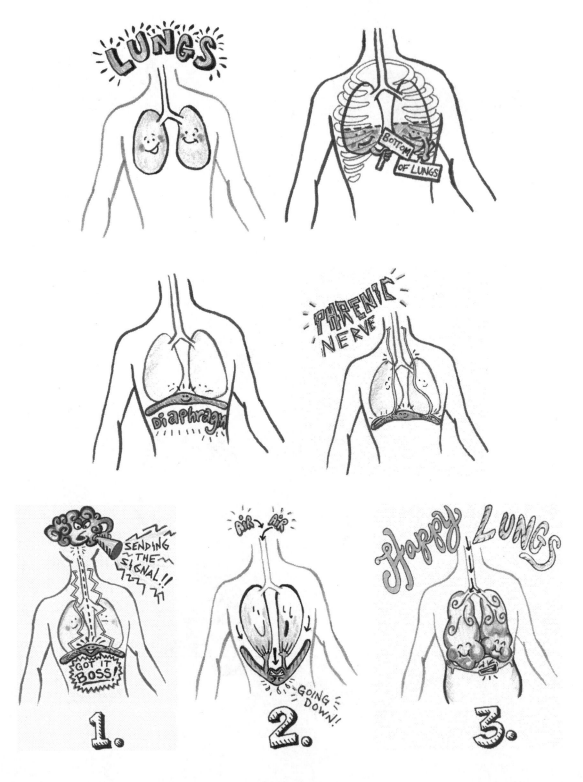

THE ECONOMICAL BREATH
The Breath – Inhale

* ECONOMICAL: Efficient without any extraneous, unnecessary effort

What can YOU do to make *The Breath – Inhale* "economical" every time?

You DON'T want to think about the phrenic nerve and the diaphragm when you breathe. They are involuntary! Let them do their work.

You DO want to think about the inhale *starting* at the bottom of the lungs, and the air *following* the diaphragm *going down – not* rising up high in the chest. Be sure to release your tummy OUT so the diaphragm can push aside the organs for the air to enter.

GIVE IT A TRY!

1. **Breathe into the bottom of your lungs:** Think of the air entering at the bottom of your lungs at the bottom of your ribcage.

2. **Release into the breath:** As you inhale, let your tummy release OUT as you guide the air to enter the bottom of your lungs and go down. That's it.

I call this the <u>Economical Breath</u> – or for our purposes – <u>The Breath</u>.

"Correct practice makes perfect." As you fall asleep at night and wake up in the morning, be aware of your tummy rising and falling with The Breath. As you go through your day, check in to see if you are in the Economical Breath/ The Breath – like when you are sitting in the car – or waiting for an elevator – or taking a walk. Is your tummy releasing out as you inhale? You don't have to be perfect – just be aware. That's a perfect start.

BODY HABITS

The Trained Dancer

And Other Reasons the Tummy Can Be Too Tight

Professional dancers often start their training as early as three years old. The discipline is to pull in the belly (and never let it go), lift and elongate the beautiful neck, and always stay pulled up. I have students who told me that their "old school" ballet teachers would hit them with a stick to reinforce *not* to breathe at the bottom of the lungs as the body desires, but to breathe at the top of the lungs to keep the beautiful line of the dancer.

Holding the tummy in is not just a habit for dancers. Do you hold your tummy in to not look fat? Or when you're working out at the gym? These all could be valid reasons! Sometimes a high breath might be what's necessary for the moment – but the fact is, it can't be for always. Even doctors have said that locking the breath can wreak havoc for your health. The Economical Breath is not only for singers and actors, but also to be a healthy human being.

Muscle memory is very strong. If you have a habit of holding your tummy in tight, chances are you are breathing the opposite way than the body requires – high in the chest. It may take some time to get comfortable with the Economical Breath, but I have a great remedy!

Changing The Channel

Singer/Actor/Human Being Channel

When I was in 7th grade, I studied Spanish with Mr. Tosca, a foreign language teacher who taught four languages at our school: Spanish, French, Italian, and German. I asked him one day, "Signor Tosca, how do you go back and forth between all of those languages? Don't you ever get mixed up?" Signor Tosca replied, "It's just like changing the channel on the television set: I change the channel, I speak another language."

This is a wonderful image for the body and the breath! If you're always breathing on *Dancer Channel* (or *Gym Channel,* or *Don't Look Fat Channel*), tell your body that you're *changing* the channel. You are now going to breathe on the *Singer/ Actor/ Human Being Channel*! Whenever you need to, you can change back.

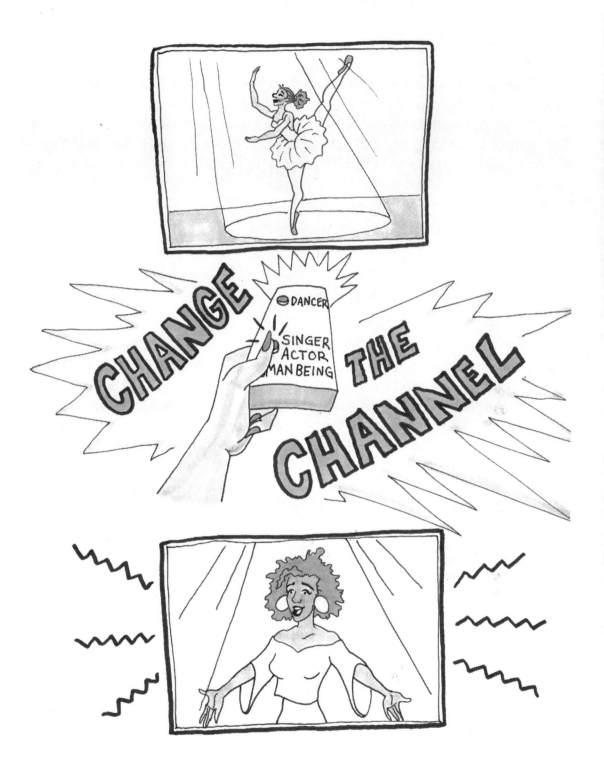

AVOIDING EMOTIONS

The Breath has a superpower, but it's not always comfortable: When you're connected to the body's natural breath, you're also directly connected to your *true* emotional life. Those feelings can range from bliss to desperation. As singers, it's our job to truthfully express those emotions in song. As human beings, however, we don't always want to be aware of those devastating emotions. It's too painful. The body remedies this uncomfortable situation by exchanging the natural Economical Breath with the high Panic Breath. The body lifts the breath above the pain and covers it with a buffer of air in the top of the lungs. The subconscious mind may be satiated for a while, happy to be avoiding the pain – but with time, something's got to give.

Anna
The Gift of Pain

"I'm in the middle of tech rehearsal for a new play," Anna told me on the phone. I had last seen my star client one year earlier. Something was troubling her, so I was glad she called. "I love the play. It's going so well. But something is going on with my breath. I can't breathe deeply." I could hear Anna wheezing. "And the other day while I was waiting for my entrance, I almost fainted right there in the wings from not being able to catch my breath. Do you have any breathing exercises for me?"

From our work together, I knew Anna had an excellent breathing technique. This sounded like a panic attack. Something was overwhelming her.

"How about we do an exercise over the phone now?" I had a notion that some emotions were well on their way to surface.

"Okay, sure," she replied.

"Lie on the floor on your back, let the floor hold you up, and breathe."

Hearing symptoms, even on the phone, is my specialty. (My friends call me the Voice Whisperer.) I could hear Anna's breath – it was high in her chest. She was gasping for air. I knew that the Panic Breath was hiding her true emotions which held the answer. "Just let the tummy rise and fall with the breath." When the sound of the high wheezing subsided, I let her breathe a bit longer. Her exhale softened.

"What are you aware of?"

"I'm going to cry." She said.

"That's good. Let it come out. Your breath is free now, and it's freeing your emotions. What are you aware of with the tears?"

(Pause)

"I'm aware that my boyfriend has been cheating on me, and it's the exact story of the play."

And there it was. The truth.

"Have you been using this story you're going through for the work?"

"No, I was using my imagination. I didn't want to go there. It's so strange that this play arrived at this time in my life."

"This play is the biggest gift you could have in your life right now," I told Anna. You are *living* the pain of the character in the play. Your body wants to go there. It needs to go there. If you take the risk to expose this truth and give it to the character, you will not only heal yourself, but you will also touch the audience at the deepest level with your intimate work. The audience won't know you're going through the same story in your life. They'll just think you're a brilliant actor! Do you think you can use this pain in your work?"

"Yes." She said.

And she did. And she could breathe again. And she got rave reviews.

> **"I always stopped breathing because I was afraid. I gave my body permission to breathe and realized that breathing protects me. It's what the body is supposed to do! It's okay not to be afraid. What is the worst thing that can happen? Breathing is LIVING! And LIVING is a beautiful thing!" – Cheutine, Actress**

Nick Can't Sing Pop
Sobbing to the Rescue

A New York Casting Director called me to help out. She explained that Nick, a young Broadway leading man, was having trouble singing in the pop style. Well – she put it more bluntly, "Nick can't sing pop!" I met him for a lesson.

Nick arrived, and I had him sing for me – the culprit – a pop song. Nick's gorgeous voice and obvious acting talent blew me away! His pop stylings? Fantastic! So, what was the problem?

Nick was breathing super high in his chest – the Panic Breath. Even though his voice was beautiful, there was so much tension in his torso that it was excruciating to watch him huff and puff and heave his upper chest. I figured the casting director was also pained by this tension and decided that *Nick can't sing pop!*

We had to get to the bottom of why Nick was breathing so high in his chest, so I had him start the hour lesson by lying on the floor on his back to get aware of his breath. Gravity is a fantastic asset for eliminating the high Panic Breath, and it worked here. Nick's very first inhale was perfect! His tummy effortlessly rose and fell with the Economical Breath. And then... tears flooded down his face.

> "What are you aware of?" I asked him.

> "I'm aware that I just went through a breakup with my fiancé." Nick started sobbing.

> "Don't clean up! Your true breath is connecting you to your true emotions. Just breathe. This is your truth today. Trust. Breathe. Be."

Nick spent the entire lesson lying on my rug, breathing, and crying for one full hour.

The next day Nick called. "That was the best lesson I've ever had!" When we worked again on connecting the Economical Breath to his singing, Nick's voice flowed effortlessly. He looked like a million bucks without any tension in sight. Now his instrument was free in every style – including pop.

The next job he booked was Judas in *Jesus Christ Superstar*.

HOLDING THE BREATH
A Common Habit

Many of us subconsciously hold our breath. Do you remember when you were in high school and didn't want the teacher to call on you in class? In order to "disappear" you held your breath. Or a time when you needed to cry but didn't dare to or it would have been too embarrassing? You held your breath.

Here are some catch phrases we say all the time that *encourage* us to hold the breath:

- Hold it together

- Keep a stiff upper lip

- Chin up

- Don't fall apart

- Hold that thought

For me, holding my breath was an old pattern from childhood. I was the "good girl" in my family. I thought there were bad emotions and good emotions: Happy was good – sad was bad. Laughing was great – getting angry was just for boys. Being gracious was a virtue – tears were too much. All of the negative feelings of pain, anger, disappointment, loss, and loneliness were bad, and I would put them away and cover them with my fabulous laugh, jovial personality, positive spirit – and – I'd hold my breath. As an adult, even though I've worked through the suppressed emotions of that sensitive little girl, at times I still have the old physical mapping of holding my breath. But, with conscious awareness and my joy of singing, I've been able to "keep breathing," even through stressful times.

It may not come as a surprise that many doctors say stress can cause physical problems by holding the breath. No wonder so many people have recurring problems like headaches, asthma, TMJ, and acid reflux.

We are so lucky to sing! I believe all singers are *required* to excavate their most painful emotions. In the work, we're not allowed to *hold it together*. We have a responsibility to breathe – and sing through it – and make it Art! Even if you're not interested in being a professional singer, this work can free your true voice, and at the same time, help you be a healthy human being.

My passion is to share this information with everybody from every walk of life. I tried to do just that with a banker.

The Banker
9/11

In New York City, only a week after the terrorist attack on the World Trade Center on September 11, 2001, I called my bank. I owned stock in one of the companies that had been housed at the World Trade Towers. The stock wasn't doing well (even before 9/11), and I was ready to sell. I spoke to a representative. When I mentioned the name of the company, he could barely speak. He was holding his breath. Even without mentioning the tragedy, I could tell this man had a personal connection with the people at this company in the World Trade Towers. Undoubtedly, he had lost dear friends and colleagues on that day. He was trying desperately to hold it together.

The representative stuttered and stammered but forged ahead as a professional working with me on the phone. He was completely unaware that every other word he said to me jolted and shook – as if he was sobbing – but he wasn't. I had the feeling this man was going to implode on the other end of the phone.

Finally, not being able to ignore it any longer, I pleaded with him, "Sir, listen to me. Go to your car today and scream at the top of your lungs. I'm an actor, so I can go to class and release all my anxiety, pain, and sorrow into my work. You don't have this outlet. If you keep holding this inside, you're going to get sick."

The man didn't interrupt me as I spoke. It's as if he was listening, but he never acknowledged what I said. He completed the transaction. I only hope he heard me.

THE SILENT BREATH

One More Tweak for the Inhale

I'm often asked about the proper way to inhale: *Do I breathe through my nose? Do I breathe through my mouth?* Yoga teachers will ask you to inhale through the nose. Others suggest mouth breathing. They all have their benefits, and none of them are against the law while singing. I say that *"singing is born out of speaking,"* and when we speak, it would be quite cumbersome to take every breath through the nose (like you're snorting). For singing, it's also cumbersome. Quick mouth inhales can promote "gasping for air." And, if a "gulp of air" rushes by your vocal cords, your cords not only get dried out, but they also blow open and must recalibrate coming back together so you can sing. Now that's cumbersome!

For our work, I'd love for you to use what I call the **Silent Breath**: Take an easy inhale through both your nose and mouth at the same time. *Imagine* that you just had a breath mint, and let the inhale feel kind of minty effervescent. In addition, as you take your Economical Breath, imagine that you can breathe through your cheeks (like through the gills of a fish). Don't make a sound. Don't open your throat (the throat stays neutral). Inhale through your nose, mouth, and cheeks – all at the same time.

That's the **Silent Breath**. It will help keep your vocal cords clear and fresh, even when you're singing for hours.

> **RELEASE INTO THE BREATH: As you inhale, try the Silent Breath breathing through your nose, mouth, and as if you could breathe through your cheeks, all at the same time. Feel the effervescent minty sensation of a breath mint. Release your tummy OUT so the diaphragm can drop down to make room for the air.**

GIVE IT A TRY!

BREATHING EXERCISE ON THE FLOOR – THE SILENT BREATH

1. Find a nice comfortable piece of floor with a mat or rug. Lie flat on the floor on your back, legs down, arms to your sides, completely releasing into the floor. Let the floor hold you up. (You have been holding yourself up all day. Now the floor will support YOU.)

2. As you lie there, take an easy **Silent Breath** inhale, and just be aware of your tummy rising and falling with the breath. Keep your eyes open (we sing with the eyes open, so it's good practice to breathe with the eyes open).

3. Don't let the air go into your upper chest. Isolate the air to enter at the bottom of the lungs. Continue to let the tummy rise and fall with the breath. This is the same, easy breath your body automatically does when you're sleeping.

BREATHING EXERCISE STANDING UP – THE SILENT BREATH

1. Stand in front of a mirror.

2. Without trying to tank up as much air a possible, take an easy **Silent Breath** inhale into the bottom of the lungs around the bottom of the rib-cage. Because the diaphragm is moving down, think of the air moving down and the tummy releasing OUT.

3. See in the mirror your tummy releasing OUT as the air enters into the bottom of your lungs.

WHAT ARE YOU AWARE OF?

Does the air want to go into the top of your lungs? Are you able to let the breath start at the bottom of the lungs with the **Silent Breath** inhale? Can you feel the difference when the air goes to the top of the lungs and when it goes to the bottom of the lungs? Don't worry about being perfect. If you can just feel the *difference* between a high breath in your chest and a low breath at the bottom of your lungs, you are on the right path! You are winning!

Are you yawning? Do you feel dizzy? If so, don't worry. That means that your old pattern of breathing was shallow. Now you are finally getting air into your system. Being dizzy is not a problem – just be sure to sit down if you're dizzy. No falling and hitting your head please! Keep breathing easily and the dizziness and yawning will dissipate. Be happy that healing air is oxygenating your system.

Are your arms tingling? Do you feel nauseous? If you're having any extreme negative reactions to inhaling an easy breath at the bottom of your lungs with your tummy releasing out and in, just lie down and keep breathing. Your body is releasing the negative emotions that have been trapped by your former breathing patterns. If you're crying, don't clean up! Keep crying! Let the emotions OUT!

Nina's Story
The Breath of Trauma

You may be wondering what happened to Nina, the enthusiastic actress with the high squeaky voice like Minnie Mouse. That day in my workshop she shared her story with the entire class that when she was a little girl, her mother tried repeatedly to commit suicide. "I went to therapy, and I realized that I've been holding my voice because of the trauma. I'd love to be able to sing and talk correctly. Can you help me?"

I was happy that Nina had already worked with a therapist. She was very aware of the issue and ready for a breakthrough. I wanted to prepare Nina as well as I could without alarming her. "Absolutely. And Nina, don't be surprised if some intense feelings come up as we work on The Breath today in class." She looked pleased. "Sound good?"

"Sounds good!"

We all stood in a circle as I explained The Breath. Then I went around the circle and checked The Breath of each student one by one. It was Nina's turn. Her high Panic Breath looked like it was strangling her. I lightly put my hands at the bottom of her ribcage. "Breathe here." Nina's chest heaved up three more times. It wasn't working. "Just trust that the breath will enter into the bottom of the lungs – just like when you sleep at night. Your body knows this breath. It wants this breath. You just have to remind it." All of the students in the circle became a part of willing this breath to come to Nina. Somehow, we all knew, without saying a word, that Nina taking a breath was a risk. It was a risk for her to be alive. All Nina could now do was to trust. Trust that her body wanted to actually breathe, wanted to live, wanted to heal. Her body resisted, but Nina did not want to avoid the pain one minute longer – the pain that she had lived with her entire childhood.

Then it came...the first correct breath at the bottom of her lungs. Tears welled up in Nina's cobalt blue eyes like crystal pearls. Her panic subsided. In silence, tears began to stream down her face.

"Hey, everyone! Nina may be crying the whole class today. Is that okay? Can you support her in that?" A resounding *YES* made Nina secure in staying open with her emotions and her newfound Breath.

Then, on the fifteen-minute break, a student told me that Nina was sick in the bathroom. I poked my head into the ladies' room and calmly inquired, "Are you okay, Nina?"

"Oh yes, I'll be right there. I'm just throwing up and having diarrhea."

(I was surprised but encouraged by Nina's calm voice.)

"Okay – good. Your body is digesting the emotions for the first time.
You are not alone in this, Nina. Just take your time."

I was breezy in my remark, hoping that Nina would find her way back to the class-room. It's very easy to say *I'm sick and I need to go home.*

To my delight, ten minutes later Nina appeared. She stayed for the entire five-hour session – crying the whole time.

The next week Nina came back for another workshop with me and was breathing 100% correctly. The poison was gone. The traumatic symptoms of vomiting and diarrhea had subsided. Her high, little girl voice came down several notches and resonated as the young woman she was.

Nina's courage and tenacity impress me to this very day. She's living her dream as a working actress, a record producer, a master teacher, and she can proudly call herself a singer.

CONFUSING PHRASES – THE BREATH

Let's revisit and decipher the seven *Confusing Phrases* from the beginning of the chapter.

CONFUSING PHRASES – THE BREATH:

1. "Breathe into your belly"
2. "Breathe into the diaphragm"
3. "Push your stomach out"
4. "Take a low, deep breath"
5. "Tank up as much air as possible"
6. "Breathe into your back"
7. Tank up like a tire around your ribs"

Let's examine each one:

1. "Breathe into your belly." Teachers use this phrase to encourage the student not to breathe into the high chest. For a Panic Breath breather, this phrase could be helpful to adjust the high breath. But there is a problem with the validity of this phrase, "Breathe into your belly": *There are no lungs in the belly.* If you try to push air into the belly instead of starting the breath at the bottom of the lungs around the ribcage, the instrument can get jammed.

   Here is the truth of what's happening in the Economical Breath:

   You breathe into the bottom of the lungs located at the bottom of the ribcage. The diaphragm drops down pushing aside the organs. Because the organs are being pushed aside by the diaphragm, the belly expands out – not because there is air in the belly.

   > *I had teachers tell me to breathe into my belly, so I thought the lungs were in my belly and tried to push air there. When I understood that the belly expands out because the diaphragm drops down and pushes the organs aside, it was a revelation! With that one little tweak, I suddenly had a higher range and more vocal ease.*

2. "Breathe into the diaphragm." There are some who think that the diaphragm fills up with air. That's just wrong. The only place the air can physically go is into the lungs.

> *Breathe into the bottom of the lungs located at the bottom of the ribcage. As an involuntary muscle, the diaphragm will do its job naturally without us thinking about it.*

3. "Push your stomach out." To push the stomach out without air entering the lungs would just be belly dancing. I prefer the command *Release into the breath:* Think of the air starting at the bottom of the lungs. Since the diaphragm is contacting *down*, think of the air entering and going *down. Release* the tummy as you inhale. The air *leads* the belly moving *out.* But for those who have been trained to hold the stomach muscles tight, like dancers, the command, "Push your stomach out," could actually be helpful to release the over-trained abdominal muscles. I used that command myself working with a young dancer on Broadway in *Billy Elliot.*

Billy Elliot on Broadway
A Dancer Who Sings

I was called by the musical supervisor of the Broadway show *Billy Elliot* to work with the boys in the cast who were playing the role of Michael. They were having trouble singing and dancing at the same time. It's always so amazing to meet young professionals like these talented boys. From an early age they know what they want to do in life. Jamie was no exception.

Jamie had been bitten by the dance bug at the tender age of six months old. His mother, a dance teacher, had brought him to one of her rehearsals when she was stuck without a babysitter. Afraid that she would have a crying baby on her hands, she put Jamie in a stroller in front of the dancers and crossed her fingers that he'd stay quiet. Not only was he quiet, but he was also completely mesmerized by the dancers, sitting still without a peep for three hours loving every minute of it. No wonder now at the age of twelve, Jamie was a top-notch skilled pro in ballet, jazz, and tap.

Jamie and the dance captain arrived at my studio. I pushed the furniture aside and folded up the rugs, giving Jamie room to sing and perform the real choreography so I could scope out the problems. Sure enough, as all trained dancers do, Jamie held his tummy tight while dancing. He tried his best to sing out the Broadway tune, but Jamie's voice got locked in his throat as he huffed and puffed high in his chest through the whole dance number. I had to find a way for Jamie to have moments where he could release his belly and take a low breath (not the Panic Breath up near the clavicles) so his voice could soar.

Jamie, the dance captain, and I slowly broke down the dance number together. We mapped out the exact moments in the choreography where Jamie could stop, release his belly, and have the breath drop *down* to the bottom of the lungs. We actually choreographed his breaths! I told Jamie clearly, *"Push your tummy out!"* He did it! With just that adjustment, Jamie's voice was immediately released. He sang without losing his breath, and, at the same time, none of the intricate and fabulous dance steps of *Billy Elliot* were compromised. (Keep in mind, only in a case like this would I use the command "Push your tummy out!" For another person it could *add* stress to their breathing.)

4. "Take a low, deep breath." If you're used to breathing at the top of your chest, or if you're a shallow breather with a tight belly like Bella Thorne, then this may be a good command for you. Just remember that you are breathing into the bottom of the lungs located at the bottom of your ribcage and not trying to push air into your belly. (There are no lungs in your stomach!) This next story highlights the "tight as a drum" breath of a military man.

Military Man
Marvin Gaye

I had the pleasure of working with Donald – a strong, sensitive, tattooed US soldier who served two tours – one in Afghanistan and one in Iraq. Upon his return from duty, Donald decided to follow his dream and pursue an acting career. He committed himself to acting classes and discovered ways to enter his emotional life that previously were off limits and never seemed accessible or appropriate as a soldier. But Donald wanted more. He wanted to play the role of Marvin Gaye – so he needed to sing.

Never having considered himself a singer, ever, he went through his fear and tried singing with me. Because of his military training, Donald's stomach muscles were as tight as a drum.

We applied my example to change the channel of his breath from *Military Channel* to *Singer/Actor/Human Being Channel*. Instantly, Donald's tight, held stomach muscles softened. He could inhale effortlessly as he applied the Economical Breath to his singing and acting. Another channel of communication was excavated and now free in his instrument. Shortly thereafter, Donald went on to successfully create his one-man show as the magnificent Marvin Gaye...and he sang! He really sang!

5. "Tank up as much as possible!" Some shallow breathers might need to think of a lot of air coming into the bottom of the lungs. But believe it or not, too much air can jam the breath. For right now, just take an easy inhale. Singing is like speaking with pitch, and when you speak, you don't need a huge breath. Sometimes a small breath is a good choice.

Jonathan
Too Much Breath

I met with Jonathan, a trained Broadway singer and dancer. With every breath he took he was trying to fill up the back of the lungs, the bottom of the lungs, even the top of the lungs. There was extra tension in his body and breathiness in his voice. (The air had to go somewhere.) Working together, I convinced Jonathan to take small, almost invisible breaths. Jonathan was suddenly singing with more ease and beauty in his voice. The unexpected side effect was that he could even send a high note longer than when he was tanking up with too much air.

6. "Breathe into your back." Because the lungs are three-dimensional, it's true that breathing from the bottom of your lungs will also fill the lungs in the front and the back. This command could be helpful for a Diva singing an extremely long and high phrase in an opera aria to get the extra air needed for the phrase. But for mere mortals, thinking about filling up the back is not necessary, and it could even add unwanted tension.

7. "Tank up like a tire around your ribs." This command gives the idea of breathing around the bottom of the ribcage and filling up the lungs sideways like a tire. When the lungs fill up around the bottom of the ribcage, there is in fact a motion that goes sideways. But because the diaphragm drops down, you should guide that downward motion with your thought that the air is going down, not sideways. Thinking to push the air sideways jams the action of the diaphragm, causing unnecessary tension.

Organize yourself... Please check off **The Breath.**

THE REVOLUTIONARY SEND

VOICE TECHNIQUE SIDE	EMOTIONAL LIFE SIDE
1. ~~The Breath~~	1. **Personalization**
2. **Support**	2. **Fourth Wall**
3. **Resonance**	3. **Sensory Condition**
4. **Floors**	4. **Need**
5. **Pyramid**	5. **Action**

We are now moving on to **Support**. This element gives you Protection, Power, and Vulnerability – and will help you have a healthy voice for life!

chapter two

SUPPORT

MARY J. BLIGE

A Superstar's Schedule – Support to the Rescue

I've always admired mega-popstar Mary J. Blige. It's no wonder I get goosebumps every time I hear her perform – she truly sings from her emotions.

I was thrilled when asked to join Mary's Creative Team as her vocal coach for a singing role in a film project in NYC. As many stars do, Mary had a hectic travel schedule and was burning the candle at both ends, flying around the country for appearances and projects. She had recently been fighting the flu, and I could tell her body was fatigued. After a full week of rehearsals with the Creative Team in New York, Mary was flying off to Los Angeles to perform on the hit TV-show *American Idol.* She was making yet another trip when she wasn't feeling 100%. I could see the worry in her eyes – Mary's voice was tired.

Before she left, I wanted to give Mary the singing tool that would be paramount in helping her with vocal fatigue, and to make sure that she would not only sing with confidence and without injuring her voice that week on *American Idol*, but that she would never lose her voice in the future: Support.

I taught Mary an easy exercise to engage the Support in the proper way. Let's do it together now: First take an easy inhale – then exhale making the sound of a snake: Say "Ssssss" with your bellybutton moving IN. Again. "Ssssss." Is your bellybutton moving IN as you say "Ssssss"? Just like Mary, you are now connecting directly to your Support.

Mary loved it. After doing the "Ssssss" exercise, we connected the Support to her voice. Before each and every phrase, Mary moved her bellybutton IN and sent out her glorious voice. Not only could she hit every powerful dynamic she wanted, but she also had full access to her signature talent – her emotions. She was on her way, feeling like she had a tool that she could count on.

Mary flew to LA, and I made sure to watch her on live TV that Monday night. I was so proud to see her bellybutton moving IN as she rocked out her song! At the same time, her voice was powerful, and her emotions completely released. She was met by a standing ovation.

The following week we were back in session. "Mary! I saw you on *American Idol.* Your bellybutton was moving IN!"

"You saw that?!" she exclaimed. "I was in the dressing room saying "Ssssss" before I went on. I was so under the weather, and it worked!"

SUPPORT
2. Voice Technique Side

SUPPORT – Exhale

The Goal: To learn how to use Support correctly, which gives you these three important results:

1. *Protection:* Protecting your vocal cords from injury
2. *Power:* Finding the true power of your personal voice
3. *Vulnerability*: Exposing your emotions while singing

Why This Is Important:

1. The right Support is imperative for vocal longevity
2. Now you can have your full vocal power *without vocal fatigue*
3. Singing with your true emotions is what makes every song magical, and moves an audience

What Has To Change: Adjust your Support to complement how the body actually works. There are many strange notions out there about how to "support" the voice, so this chapter is important.

"How do you think about Support for singing?"

I ask each new student what they have been taught, or what they have heard about Support.

The following phrases are some of the answers I often hear. Are these commands true or false? (Spoiler alert: They are all false.)

CONFUSING PHRASES – SUPPORT:

1. "Support from your diaphragm"
2. "Hold your stomach really hard"
3. "Clench your buttocks"
4. "Push your stomach out to support as you sing"
5. "Hold your ribs out"
6. "You can't have too much Support"

Let's revisit these *Confusing Phrases* at the end of the chapter. First, let's make sense of Support.

SUPPORT – Exhale

I think there is an epidemic of *no Support* in our society for speaking, and there is an epidemic of *no Support* for singers. Vocal protection, power, and vulnerability are essential in our lives – and that comes from Support.

Before we learn how to connect Support to your voice, let's get even more clear about what Support is.

Making Sense of Support – What does Support mean?

SUPPORTING FROM UNDERNEATH

Where is the Support of a building?

In New York City, I live on the 16th floor of a 22-floor high-rise. If the support system of my building were up on my 16th floor, what would happen? The building would topple over! So, where is the Support of my building? That's right – in the *foundation* at the *bottom* of the building. Fortunately, my building *does* have the Support in the foundation – so the other tenants and I are safe.

In singing, you need to think of your *entire body* as your instrument (not just the vocal cords). Let's take a moment to think of your body as my building in New York: At the top of the building, you have the phrenic nerve, the lungs, and the diaphragm. They are doing their involuntary work to make the body breathe.

▌ *The phrenic nerve, lungs, and diaphragm must be free to do their work.*

Just like my 16th floor apartment, for both talking and singing, we don't want the Support to be at the *top* of the building. Think of the skyscrapers in San Francisco and Japan. Architects design those tall buildings so that during an earthquake the tops of the buildings will sway with the motion of the tremors. The strong foundation at the bottom of the buildings with the flexible structure at the top save the high-rises from crashing down. That's a perfect image for our Support technique. The neck, shoulders, and upper abdominals that surround the lungs and diaphragm must be supple and free. Any added muscle tension from trying to support "on top" would jam the whole works.

Instead of the Support being at the top of your instrument, the Support must come from underneath – *below* the lungs, and *below* the diaphragm. What is below the diaphragm?

THE BELLYBUTTON!

The bellybutton is where you will always <u>initiate</u> the Support.

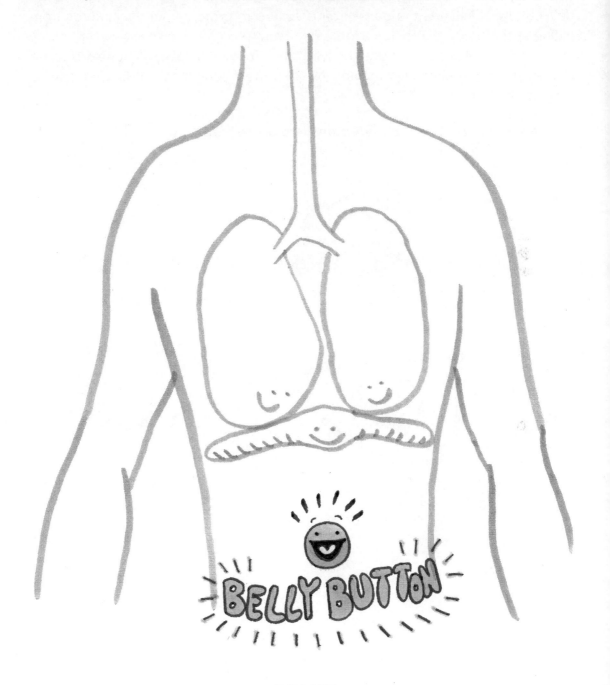

1. SUPPORT AS PROTECTION

The correct Support for both talking and singing is the same Support the body already knows and wants to protect the vocal cords. That's right – there is a system already in place in your body that will keep your vocal cords protected.

For example, think of sneezing: When you exhale with a sneeze, **your body pulls your bellybutton IN** without your even knowing it. Why? This action of moving the bellybutton IN initiates the *correct air pressure* to protect your vocal cords from hitting each other with too much force. Try it now – pretend to sneeze: *Aaaa-choo!* On *"choo,"* you'll notice that your bellybutton is moving IN! We will hone this same movement – the bellybutton moving IN – to protect your vocal cords when speaking and singing.

I call the Support "Super Bellybutton!" – a Superhero!

What happens if you don't protect the vocal cords with the proper Support?

In the short run, incorrect Support can bring on vocal fatigue. Suddenly, speaking and singing feel like more of a strain, but you don't know why. Long term, a nodule or a polyp can form on the vocal folds, which has brought many a singing career to a halt. Just as bad, without the correct Support, the vocal cords can hemorrhage, as small blood vessels in the cords rupture.

Hemorrhaged Vocal Cords

In an interview early in her career, I heard a famous young singer say she had experienced a sudden attack of laryngitis. She attributed the attack to having "pushed" her voice to be heard over her band that particular evening. For me, the word "pushed" is a red flag regarding Support. Not being connected to the Bellybutton Support and pushing from the throat can indeed bring on acute laryngitis — and if the Support is not corrected, more vocal damage is possible.

Soon after that interview, she set out on her first concert tour. In the middle of the tour something terrible happened: Her vocal cords hemorrhaged. She had to cancel the balance of the tour and recover. Fortunately, the singer reported that she found a wonderful surgeon. Months later, having had the operation to mend her vocal cords, she said that her voice felt and sounded better than ever. She had officially recovered.

Before she went back out for a second tour, I watched a television special of her singing some of her new material for a live television audience with her "new" voice. I watched intently as she sang. I was able to identify a potential source of her previous injury which she had not yet corrected: She was not using her correct Support. Instead of scooping the bellybutton IN as she sang, I observed the action of her abdomen pushing DOWN. This action *jams* the Support, and with time, hinders the health of the vocal cords.

She did go back out for a second tour — and her vocal cords hemorrhaged again. She had to cancel her tour for a second time.

A good surgeon can often fix the damaged vocal cords, but if the problem of *how* the injury occurred in the first place is not remedied — in this case, incorrect Support — the damage will recur.

SCOOPING FROM THE BELLYBUTTON

The Swing

When you initiate the exhale from the bellybutton moving IN, think of a "scooping motion" going in and curving up like a SWING, as you say "Ssssss." It's just an easy swinging motion in.

Why the swinging motion?

- As you INHALE, the **diaphragm is working involuntarily** by contracting down to create a vacuum in the lungs so the air can rush in — at the same time, the belly and bellybutton release OUT

- As you EXHALE with the "Ssssss," **YOU are working**, bringing the abs around the bellybutton IN as the diaphragm relaxes and rises back up to its home underneath the lungs

- As you swing the bellybutton IN on "Ssssss," **you are following the diaphragm** rising back up to its resting place underneath the lungs — The air pressure energy of your "Ssssss" is *leading* the motion of the swing

- The swinging motion that follows the diaphragm as it rises back up to its home underneath the lungs, gives you the most synchronized action possible with the most economical results — easy Support

"Ssssss" SUPPORT EXERCISE — THE SWING

GIVE IT A TRY!

- Stand in front of a mirror

- Take your easy **Silent Breath** inhale at the bottom of the lungs — let the tummy release OUT so the air can enter

- Now on the exhale, just like Mary J. Blige did, SWING your bellybutton IN, and SEND the sound of a snake, "Ssssss"

- Do that a few times

> **Remember, don't let the upper abdominals around the lungs and diaphragm clutch, hold, or be a part of the Support. Those muscles must remain supple so the diaphragm can do its work without interference.**

THE STERNUM POPPING OUT

As your bellybutton swings IN on the "Ssssss," notice in the mirror that at the same time your sternum is popping OUT. You won't necessarily *feel* the sternum popping out, but you can see it in the mirror as proof it's happening.

- Repeat the "Ssssss" Exercise in the mirror — Make sure you see your sternum popping OUT when the bellybutton swings IN on "Ssssss"

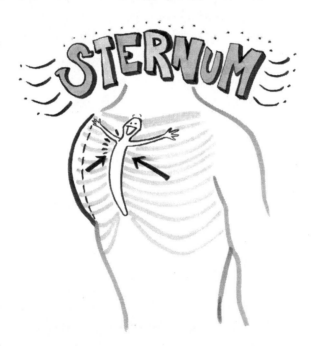

WHAT ARE YOU AWARE OF?

Can you see in the mirror the bellybutton swinging IN and your sternum popping OUT? If you can, that's it! It means that your upper torso is free, and The Breath and Support are in place.

If you can't see your sternum popping out in the mirror when you say "Ssssss," think of initiating the swinging motion one inch below the bellybutton. If you're short waisted or long waisted, one inch below the bellybutton could give you more swinging power. It should be a buoyant wonderful feeling when your bellybutton scoops IN on each exhale and your sternum pops OUT as you say "Sssssss."

"Ssssss" LYING ON THE FLOOR

GIVE IT A TRY!

1. Just as you did with the breathing exercise in Chapter One, you're going to lie on the floor – but first, find a mirror or something reflective to set up next to you low to the floor.

2. Now lie down on your back, legs down, arms to your sides, completely releasing into the floor. Let the floor hold you up. Keep your eyes open as you lie there (we sing with our eyes open, so it's good practice).

3. **Be aware of your tummy rising and falling with the breath.**

4. On the next inhale, let the tummy rise.

5. Then as you exhale, **say "Ssssss," and scoop your bellybutton IN**. While the bellybutton swings IN, the lower abdominal muscles around the area of the bellybutton are engaged, also moving IN and "sending" – never holding or clutching like you might do for a sit-up.

CHECK THE STERNUM IN A MIRROR

1. As you lie on the floor, now turn your head and look at the reflection of your upper torso.

2. As you exhale on the "Ssssss" initiating from the bellybutton, watch your sternum.

3. The sternum releases OUT as the bellybutton moves IN. Observe the motion in the reflection.

WHAT ARE YOU AWARE OF?

Did you see in the mirror your sternum popping OUT as your bellybutton moved IN? If YES, this means your upper torso is released! You are successful in connecting The Breath with the Support without any extra tension. Your upper abs are loose so the lungs and the diaphragm can do the work as the body requires. The lower abs around the bellybutton are the muscles that are working. If it feels easier, try initiating the "Ssssss" one inch below the bellybutton. The adjustment may be better for your body type.

QUICK "Sss" LYING ON THE FLOOR

GIVE IT A TRY!

1. Now take a little breath and exhale on a short "Sss."

2. Repeat that in a quick rhythm: short inhale – exhale "Sss" – short inhale – exhale "Sss" – etc...

3. On each inhale your tummy will release out as the air enters your lungs.

4. On the exhale, the bellybutton bounces in with each short "Sss."

5. Turn your head to look at your reflection. Notice that with each short exhale your sternum is bouncing up. This is proof that you are supporting correctly, and your upper body is in the release!

WHAT ARE YOU AWARE OF?

Do you like the exercise lying on the floor? Is it easier to connect to your Breath and Support? This Floor Exercise can be ideal because the earth's gravity helps us release the body into the floor with no extraneous tension.

Take advantage of the times when you are lying down – like before you fall asleep and when you wake up in the morning. Your body will be in its natural state, and you can observe your breathing with your tummy effortlessly rising and falling with the breath. If you get the chance to see a baby awake or asleep, check their breathing – it's always correct! Watch someone sleeping or taking a catnap. If the person snores, even better! You can observe the tummy rising on the inhale, and then the bellybutton moving IN on the exhale which engages the Support for their vocal snoring. What a fun way to see your voice technique in action!

2. SUPPORT AS POWER

The *movement* of the bellybutton scooping IN is the effort that gives you the *power* of your voice – not the vocal cords and not the diaphragm. They are the *receivers* of the powerful bellybutton swinging IN. You must keep the *upper* abdominals (around the ribcage) supple and free so the lungs and diaphragm can do their work without any hindrance from muscle tension. If you squeeze or push from the diaphragm to support, the whole system will fall apart.

Sidney Poitier
Don't Squeeze the Diaphragm

From his best-selling autobiography, *Measure of a Man*, one of my favorite actors, icon Sidney Poitier, describes his own personal experience in his early acting years being told to take diaphragm lessons. Disaster!

"While I wasn't home yet in the truly professional sense, I was a long way from those early times back in the theatrical woods when I was told by fellow inexperienced actors and by some not very good drama teachers, 'You have to take diaphragm lessons. You have to be able to speak from your diaphragm so that you can be heard up in the last row of the theatre. You must learn to bring your voice from the diaphragm, push it up, squeeze it out so that it will resound into the audience.'

"Well, I almost squeezed myself to death trying to be heard in the balcony. I'm serious. I was constipated during half my early performances. My stomach was always in one of those Canadian isometric exercises. I mean it was like a knot, I developed such muscles around my diaphragm from squeezing everything out of me all the time." – Sidney Poitier

> **"The diaphragm is a God given muscle. It works automatically. You don't have to think about it. Just know where it is. God gave it to you. It's a miracle."**
> **– Mrs. Mitchell, drama teacher at Emerson College**

3. SUPPORT AS VULNERABILITY

Support connects you to your vulnerability. How? Baby's first scream is powerful, emotional, and in the perfect Support. Trust that when you are connected to the correct Breath and Support, you are also lining up your body as the vessel to your true vulnerability.

Joe's Vulnerability
I Squeak Like a Little Girl

A young actor from Australia called me to work on his speaking and singing voice. He used to have nodules on his vocal cords. The doctor said that the nodules were now gone from resting his voice, but Joe wisely wanted to make sure he wasn't continuing with the bad habits that gave him the nodules in the first place. He told me that when he got emotional his voice would "squeak like a little girl" – not what Joe wanted in his acting or in his life.

After examining Joe's voice technique, I wasn't surprised that his Support was completely jammed. Every muscle in his body was holding on. This "tight as a drum" extra pressure could indeed make a man's voice go from a natural deep resonance to a sudden, unexpected, "squeaky" falsetto – especially when he was emotional. "Are you an athlete?" I inquired. The mystery was unveiled:

"As a teenager, I always felt like a small, weak person, without any physical power," Joe shared. "I pushed myself to get strong. I became the goalie on my high school soccer team. When the team workout was done, I'd stay after, put on full body pads and my buddy would throw soccer balls at me as hard as he could."

Even though Joe's self-imposed, masochistic workouts had been a decade before, his body still held the muscle memory in his nervous system to "tighten every-thing!" Now, when Joe got emotional and vulnerable, unconscious gripping would take over, and his voice would *squeak*.

Joe and I got to work to change the "software" of his system. Softening the upper abs added power to his lower abs. Releasing his shoulders and neck made his body surrender. His *Super Bellybutton* served as his point of power. The *squeaking little girl* departed, and a strong, vulnerable man took her place.

Joe found boxing and martial arts, which went hand in hand with our breathing work! The instructor showed him the power of synergy and release, using muscle power *with* the breath. Never again would Joe "tighten everything."

Because of his commitment to boxing, martial arts, and his new voice technique, we were able to do away with the old mapping Joe developed as a teen. Joe's voice connected beautifully, and he no longer had the embarrassment of his voice *squeaking* when he got emotional. And the best side effect – the nodules on his vocal cords never came back.

I will always be asking you to initiate the Support from the bellybutton. The bellybutton is underneath the lungs and underneath the diaphragm to act as the Support of your instrument – your voice. One may also ruminate on the fact that the bellybutton is where you were attached to your mother by the umbilical cord. It's the zone where you think from your "gut." It's a place of your power and vulnerability. The bellybutton will serve you well.

TRY IT AGAIN!

"Ssssss" STANDING

- Take an easy inhale with the **Economical Breath**
- As you exhale, with the sound of "Ssssss" SWING the bellybutton IN

Be sure not to hold the stomach muscles like you might do in a sit-up. The bellybutton keeps swinging IN on the entire exhale "Ssssss" – then inhale – exhale "Ssssss" – then inhale – exhale "Ssssss," etc.

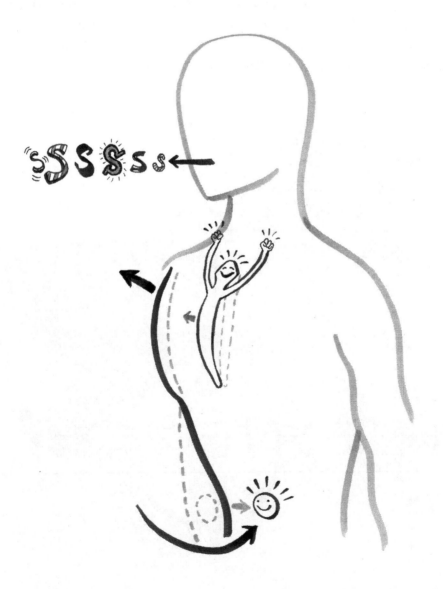

SING

TONGUE TRILL & LIP TRILL

You are not singing yet, but let's add the voiced Tongue Trill and Lip Trill to keep practicing your Support.

1. TONGUE TRILL

Can you roll your tongue like an Italian [r]? Say *Bravo! Brrrrrravo!*

Now roll the [r]: **"Drrrrr"**

As you say **"Drrrrr,"** bring your hands in front of your bellybutton. Make a hand-over-hand circling motion, like a basketball referee motioning the signal for the foul "walking/traveling." Give it a try! Say **"Drrrrr"** while circling your hands:

"Drrrrr"

Some English speakers have trouble rolling the [r] saying **"Drrrrr."** If it's difficult for you, you can substitute the Tongue Trill with the Lip Trill in the exercises ahead.

2. LIP TRILL

Have you ever seen a child make the sound of a car engine with their lips? Two lips vibrate together, the voice is added and...ta-da! It's the sound of a rumbling engine. Give it a try: **"Brrrrr"**

As you are saying **"Brrrrr,"** bring your hands in front of your bellybutton. Make a hand-over-hand circling motion, like a basketball referee motioning the signal for "walking/traveling." Give it a try! Say **"Brrrrr"** while circling your hands.

"Brrrrr"

If you are having a hard time getting your lips to move, forego the referee motion for a moment. Take your two index fingers and push UP on either side of your mouth. This makes your lips and cheeks more fleshy. Try again. **"Brrrrr"**

Now with your Tongue and Lip Trills ready, we'll add one more wonderful image to keep in mind as you're circling your hands for the following Support exercises:

TWO BALLS SPINNING AROUND EACH OTHER

The thought of *two balls spinning around each other* gives you the image and sensation of a spinning propeller of energy as you circle your hands and swing your bellybutton Support IN.

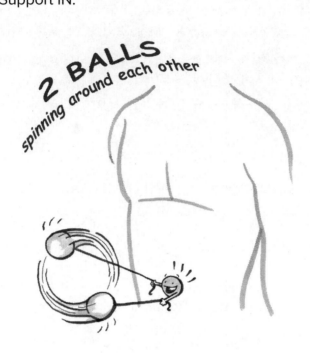

This is an added image for the Support to help you keep *moving* the bellybutton IN – not *holding*. That's one of the reasons why my method is called *The Revolutionary SEND*, not *The Revolutionary HOLD*.

TONGUE TRILL EXERCISE – "Drrrrr"

GIVE IT A TRY!

FIRST DO THE "Ssssss" EXERCISE

- Stand in front of a mirror – take an easy **Economical Breath** inhale at the bottom of the lungs – see your tummy release OUT in the mirror

- Then swing the bellybutton IN and say "Ssssss" – see in the mirror your sternum popping OUT as the bellybutton scoops IN

- Repeat

"Drrrrr" EXERCISE

- Take an easy inhale – **The Breath** – see your tummy release OUT in the mirror

- Bring your hands in front of your bellybutton – make a hand-over-hand circling motion as you swing your bellybutton IN while saying "Drrrrr"

- Imagine your circling hands are *the two balls spinning around each other* with the energy of a propeller – **"Drrrrrr"**

- See in the mirror your sternum popping OUT as the bellybutton scoops IN *leading* the Tongue Trill – **"Drrrrrr"**

- Repeat

WHAT ARE YOU AWARE OF?

Is it fun to circle your hands as you swing your bellybutton IN while saying "Drrrrr?" Be sure the bellybutton is swinging IN. The propeller energy of the image of *two balls spinning around each other* is LEADING the vibration of your Tongue Trill. Don't push from your tongue – let the bellybutton motion swinging IN be the force that's trilling your tongue. It should feel easy!

LIP TRILL EXERCISE – "Brrrrr"

GIVE IT A TRY!

FIRST DO THE "Ssssss" EXERCISE

- Take an easy inhale – The Breath – see your tummy release OUT in the mirror

- Exhale initiating the "Ssssss" from the bellybutton swinging IN – See your sternum popping OUT as the bellybutton scoops IN

- Repeat

"Brrrrr" EXERCISE

- Take an easy inhale – The Breath – see your tummy release OUT in the mirror

- Bring your hands in front of your bellybutton – make a hand-over-hand circling motion as you swing your bellybutton IN while saying "Brrrrr"

- Imagine your circling hands are *the two balls spinning around each other* with the energy of a propeller – **"Brrrrrr"**

- See in the mirror your sternum popping OUT as the bellybutton scoops IN *leading* the Lip Trill – **"Brrrrrr"**

- Repeat

WHAT ARE YOU AWARE OF?

Are your lips trilling? Be sure the bellybutton is swinging IN with the energy of *two balls spinning around each other* like a propeller. The energy of the bellybutton scooping IN is LEADING the vibration of your Lip Trill. Don't engage the upper abs around the ribcage and diaphragm – this will jam the instrument, hindering the involuntary work of the diaphragm muscle. Remember Sidney Poitier's stomach in knots.

Do you feel extra air escaping? If there is extra air in the sound, you may be opening your throat and blowing air from the back to make the lips trill. If you have this extra air, think of "closing the door" in the back of your throat. Of course, I don't mean to add tension to your throat! You are just shutting off the open space in the back of your throat so there no extraneous air. You'll feel solid vibration in the *front* of your mouth, and the lips will vibrate easily.

Are you still having trouble trilling your lips? If so, forego circling your hands for a moment. Take your two index fingers and push UP on either side of your mouth to make the lips and cheeks more fleshy. Try again. For many it's a favorite exercise – but for others it's not so easy. I suggest you keep trying it daily. But there will be other exercises you can go to if it's not your preference.

MYTH: "If your lips don't trill, it's because your mouth and jaw are tense." Actually, if your lips don't trill, it's most likely because you are not connected to your Support. The bellybutton must be scooping IN like a swing. The moving energy like two balls spinning around each other is the force that is leading your lips to vibrate.

ADDING THE BELLYBUTTON-DOWN

Your Leg Energy is Also a Part of the Support

Now that you are an expert swinging your bellybutton IN, we will add one more tweak to your Support – your legs – which I call *Bellybutton-Down*. Don't worry, you don't have to hold your legs tight or think about what some people call "grounding." You do *not* want to be stuck in the ground. Some of the high-rise buildings in San Francisco are built on rollers in the foundation so the entire building moves, including the base! (My friend told me he was caught in a San Francisco tremor in one of those buildings, and it was a *wild ride!*) You can be sure that movement helps with Support!

Instead of holding the legs tight, you just want to make sure the energy in your lower body is moving and active. In this exercise you're going to bend your knees and feel a *buoyant* energy in your legs.

GIVE IT A TRY!

LIP TRILL EXERCISE – ADD A KNEE BEND AS YOU TRILL YOUR LIPS

- As your bellybutton moves IN on the Lip Trill, bend your knees – The leg energy is also a part of your Support

- When you drop down into the knee bend, nod your head "yes" as you trill your lips – That motion will make sure your neck muscles are not clutching

- Now you are TRAINING the body that the Bellybutton-Down is the Support of your instrument, and the neck and upper torso are free without tension

TRY IT AGAIN!

- Bellybutton moves IN as you do the Lip Trill

- Bend your knees (you can really bounce them) as the bellybutton moves IN

- As you drop down into the knee bend, nod your head "yes" and release the neck and upper torso

Carrie's Legs
Wheelchair to Standing

Because of a motorcycle accident, Carrie was in a wheelchair for a year. I've had several students who are confined to wheelchairs. It's possible to sing in every position, including only sitting down. In Carrie's case, the doctors didn't know if she was ever going to walk again. But after eleven operations and an unstoppable determination, Carrie was walking. Now it was time for Carrie to follow her true passion – to act. She decided to take on the triple threat performer Ann Margret as a one-woman show. Not only was Carrie acting, but as Ann Margret, she had the demand to sing and dance! Carrie had never trained for singing and dancing before the accident – and now she was learning new skills while her body was still healing. Carrie called me to be her voice teacher, and we got to work.

Because of the accident, Carrie's body learned to survive in the wheelchair using only the strength of her head, neck, and shoulders, while her legs remained dormant in order to heal. Now that she was out of the wheelchair standing, the old muscle memory of a year in the wheelchair remained: Carrie's sensation of *Bellybutton-Down* was completely non-existent. It was imperative for me to help Carrie to re-map her body's balance to give the Support to her bellybutton and legs, and to release the upper torso.

Carrie shared with me how difficult it was and how patient she had to be with letting the neck muscles really go. I reminded her that during the time in the wheelchair, the neck and upper body muscles gave her life. They became her legs. Now those same muscles had to regroup and understand that the extra work was not needed anymore. She has beautiful legs, and they will take over now for the Support.

With time and patience, Carrie made a full recovery! Her *Bellybutton-Down* Support was in place, and her legs were in action. Carrie sang and she danced!

Her one-woman show was a HIT and garnered rave reviews.

TRILL YOUR LIPS AGAIN!

ADD KNEE BEND AND NOD YOUR HEAD "YES"

- Take an easy inhale – **The Breath**
- On the exhale **Support**, your bellybutton moves IN
- Send out the Lip Trill and bend your knees (you can really bounce them) as the bellybutton moves IN
- As you drop down into the knee bend, nod your head "yes" looking down at the floor to release the neck and upper torso

WHAT ARE YOU AWARE OF?

Are your lips buzzing? Be sure that the bellybutton is scooping IN and actually leading the vibration of your lips. *Don't try to push the lips.* If your lips are not buzzing, it probably means you are not scooping the bellybutton in with enough support energy. The bellybutton leads the Lip Trill – not the other way around.

TRY IT AGAIN!

If you are still having difficulty getting the lips to trill, you can cheat a little by putting your index fingers underneath and to the sides of the corners of your mouth and pushing up. This creates more flesh around the mouth, so you'll have an easier time trilling those lips.

Be sure not to "blow" air from the back of your throat. The throat needs to be in its natural state – not opening too wide. You'll feel solid vibration in the *front* of your mouth, and the lips will vibrate easily.

WHAT ARE YOU AWARE OF?

Are your lips trilling now? Bend your knees and nod your head "yes" as you trill your lips. Keep SENDING and swinging the bellybutton IN like two balls spinning around each other.

MUSCLE VS. FAT

THE TRADITIONAL OPERA SINGER
Is it better to be fat than thin to be a great singer?

Traditional opera singers have always been stereotyped as big and round. Does that mean it's better to be fat to be a great singer?

SUPPORT

In one respect, having more fat can be an advantage for singing. As we now know, to support the voice, the abdominal muscles around the bellybutton are engaged and move IN. As I have repeated over and over, it's important to *not hold* these muscles tight. The bellybutton must move IN with the energy of two balls spinning around each other.

Here's an interesting physical truth: A singer with more fat in the area of the bellybutton can pull the tummy IN as hard as they can — and never overdo it. It's physically *impossible* to grab the muscles too tightly because the layer of fat serves to cushion the movement — the stomach muscles can't physically grab.

On the other hand, a singer with all muscle and little fat, can constrict the Support by holding the muscles too tight. If you are slender and have strong abdominal muscles from sit-ups and exercise, be especially conscious *not to grip* the lower ab muscles around the bellybutton. Be sure to *send* and *not hold*. If you have belly-fat, enjoy! Use that Support!

CONFUSING PHRASES – SUPPORT

Let's revisit the *Confusing Phrases* from the beginning of the chapter. Many of these phrases are popular, but all of them are wrong.

CONFUSING PHRASES – SUPPORT:

1. "Support from your diaphragm"
2. "Hold your stomach really hard"
3. "Clench your buttocks"
4. "Push your stomach out to support as you sing"
5. "Hold your ribs out"
6. "You can't have too much Support"

Let's examine each one:

1. "Support from your diaphragm." This phrase is so popular that it's like an old folklore saying. But it's confusing: You are not supporting *from* the diaphragm. You are instead supporting from *underneath* the diaphragm. I call it Bellybutton-Down. Don't forget Sidney Poitier squeezing his diaphragm into a knot! NOT!

2. "Hold your stomach really hard." Holding your stomach "really hard" just gives you tension everywhere. Do not *hold* the Support. While singing we must always SEND.

> *Don't "hold" the tummy. Instead, you initiate every whisper, scream, or song by swinging the bellybutton IN. Do this, and you'll keep your voice healthy.*

AMY THE ROCKETTE

My student Amy was in the best shape of anyone I knew. She was a Broadway dancer, a Dance Captain at Radio City Music Hall with the Rockettes, and taught Pilates. Because of all her dance training, not surprisingly, Amy was having difficulty with her singing Support. To check her technique, I had Amy lie on her back on the floor to do the "Ssssss" exercise. As she was bringing the bellybutton IN for her exhale, the upper abs were also clutching. Her dance training required Amy to hold in all her abdominal muscles, both upper and lower. It was a new practice for Amy to not have the upper abs engaged.

"Oh my goodness, the abs around my bellybutton are getting so tired! Is that right?" she exclaimed.

"Yes, it is!" I replied. "As long as the motion from the bellybutton is *moving in* and *not holding*, it is right."

I was surprised that even though Amy was in magnificent shape as a dancer, the motion of moving the bellybutton in *without* clutching the upper abs was in fact physically taxing at first. Her bellybutton was tired! With a little time, it was easy. Singing is also athletic training!

3. "Clench your buttocks." I call it *Bellybutton-Down* for your Support, and the buttocks are down – however, clenching your buttocks tight is just holding tension. Try clenching your buttocks right now. Notice that your throat gets tight immediately. You don't want a tight throat while singing, so please, don't clench your buttocks for Support.

4. "Push your stomach out to support as you sing." This is the opposite of what the body does to support. Try it yourself now. Do an "Sssss" as you push your stomach out. Do you feel tension around your neck and in your throat? That's the last place you want tension!

   ▌ *Bring the bellybutton IN as you support. Don't push the belly out.*

5. "Hold your ribs out." When you breathe into the bottom of your lungs, you can see in a mirror the ribcage expanding. This is a consequence of the diaphragm dropping down to make room for the air. The question is, as you are exhaling, should you *hold* the ribs *out* to help support the breath? If you are *holding* the ribs *out*, you are actually adding exterior tension around the lungs and hindering the diaphragm from doing its involuntary work.

6. "You can't have too much Support." As you will see in some of the exercises ahead to sing high notes, the energy of the Support does indeed change throughout the range of your voice. If you think "support as much as possible at all times," it doesn't work. And, if you are trying to support with *all* the abdominal muscles, the tension around the lungs and the diaphragm will jam everything.

Organize yourself... Please check off **Support**.

THE REVOLUTIONARY SEND

VOICE TECHNIQUE SIDE	EMOTIONAL LIFE SIDE
1. ~~The Breath~~	1. **Personalization**
2. ~~Support~~	2. **Fourth Wall**
3. **Resonance**	3. **Sensory Condition**
4. **Floors**	4. **Need**
5. **Pyramid**	5. **Action**

Next up – **Resonance**. This element unlocks the sound of your true, one-of-a-kind voice.

chapter three

RESONANCE

KERRY WASHINGTON
Singing is Born Out of Speaking

Kerry Washington reached out to me – not for singing lessons, but to help her with her speaking voice. She had the demand of performing eight shows a week on Broadway in the gripping play by Christopher Demos-Brown, *American Son*. When we think of well-known actors starring on Broadway, it always sounds so glamorous – the fame, the opportunity to do ones' craft in front of a lot of people. But this ambitious work is an art form, and performing eight shows a week is not for the meek. Kerry Washington is like an Olympic athlete when it comes to her acting preparation. She leaves nothing to chance, working out her body, her mind, and her emotions. For our work, Kerry wanted to make sure she could dive into the extreme emotions of her character, Kendra Ellis-Connor – the mother of a missing biracial teenager – and never lose her voice.

Of course, the first two elements, The Breath and Support, must be in place – and Kerry nailed those perfectly. Then it was time to hookup The Breath and Support with her *voice*. Kerry insisted on *not* singing, so I had fun giving her exercises to find that tickling, effortless vibration around her mouth and lips, which I call The Front Passage resonators. We did exercises like lip trills, tongue trills, and another exercise where I told her to speak as if the words lived in her cheeks. During the exercises, I asked Kerry if she knew the song "Moon River." "Oh yes," she said, "it's from one of my favorite movies, *Breakfast at Tiffany's*." I stood on one side of the studio and threw an imaginary ball of vibration to her, saying, "*Mooooon Riiiiiver*." She'd throw the imaginary ball back to me, "*Mooooon Riiiiiver*." Then, as sneaky as I could be, I started to add pitch to the words – the very notes that Henry Mancini wrote, "*Mooooon Riiiiiiver*." Kerry played along and sung it back, "*Mooooon Riiiiiiver*." Then, I continued, "*Wiiiider than a mile*." "I know what you're doing!" she needled me. "Yep," I grinned, "Now your singing!" And let me tell you, her voice was gorgeous.

This was the perfect example of my adage *"singing is born out of speaking."* Adding singing to Kerry's daily warm-up before the play gave her a vibrant, personal, home base resonator — the Front Passage — so that she could speak, yell, scream, cry, whisper, whatever the character called for, with the effortless power of Resonance that would carry to the back of the house eight shows a week.

Kerry Washington received rave reviews for her role, and never missed a performance. May her next Broadway show be a musical!

RESONANCE

3. Voice Technique Side

RESONANCE – Your Voice

The Goal: To learn how to activate the Resonance of your personal vocal sounding board – what I call the Front Passage – for both speaking and singing.

Why This Is Important: This is how you access your unique, healthy, one-of-a-kind voice.

What Has To Change: You might be surprised that the vibration necessary to resonate your voice in a healthy manner doesn't come from your throat where your vocal cords live. Speaking or singing in your throat can bring on "vocal fry," that scratchy, bacon sizzling sound that happens when your vocal cords rub together. Learning how to activate your Front Passage resonators will keep your speaking voice healthy and make you the singer you were born to be.

"What have you heard about Resonance?"

I ask each new student what they have been taught, or what they've heard about Resonance.

The following phrases are some of the answers I often hear. Some of them are correct, some are incorrect, but all of them need further explanation for healthy speaking and great singing.

CONFUSING PHRASES – RESONANCE:

1. "Sing into the Mask"
2. "Place your voice forward"
3. "Sing into your nose"
4. "Open your throat"
5. "Sing in your throat"

We will revisit these *Confusing Phrases* at the end of the chapter. First, let's learn about Resonance and what healthy speaking and great singing are all about!

RESONANCE – YOUR VOICE
The Connection

Now it is time to connect The Breath and the Support with *your voice*! So, the question is, how do you do that? What *is* your voice? How do you *think* about your voice?

Let's begin with what not to think about.

DON'T THINK ABOUT YOUR VOCAL CORDS
The Quantum Theory

It's true, you have vocal cords in your throat, and without them you wouldn't have a voice. They are a gift at birth. Your vocal cords vibrate and have a unique, one-of-a-kind sound that is yours.

And yet, for your voice technique, *thinking* about your vocal cords when speaking or singing impedes your natural voice. I've always known this from experience, but then one day my student connected the concept to science.

"If you think about your vocal cords and try to *tell* them what to do with your mind, the cords freak out," I said to my student Matt during his first voice lesson.

"Mary, you're right!" Matt exclaimed, "I study physics – and it's true!" My eyes widened with delight as I listened to Matt prove my point. "In physics, quantum theory says that when you observe a molecule, it changes the state of that molecule. Therefore, if we think about the vocal cords, they will not be in their natural state for speaking and singing." What a light bulb moment! *Thank you, Matt!*

Quantum theory helps us to understand our voice technique: We don't want to observe and thus change the natural state of our vocal cords. We want the cords to be free to do their job naturally without any extraneous effort.

Where do you put your attention?

I'll let you in on a secret: You are now going to think of *your voice* as Resonance.

The human body can resonate the voice in many ways – namely the head, throat, and chest. Instead of putting your attention on the vocal cords and the other areas in your body that vibrate and add Resonance to your sound, you will now focus on what I call the **dominant resonator** of your voice – **The Front Passage**.

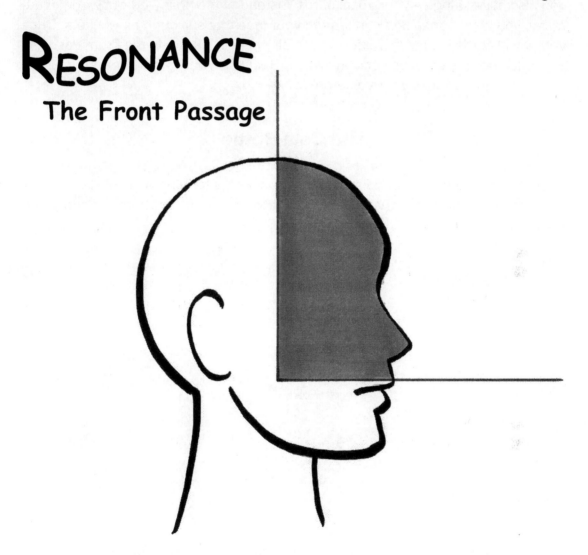

The Front Passage is the area in your face located from your upper lip and in front of your ears going straight up. This "passage" in your head is like the sounding board in a piano. The Front Passage houses the resonators or "speakers" of your voice.

The Guitar

Think of your voice for a moment like a guitar: A guitar has strings, and is made of high-quality wood that is hollowed out inside, creating a large air pocket. After the strings are struck, that air pocket of the guitar vibrates against the rich wood and sends out the one-of-a-kind timbre of that guitar.

You also have strings – your vocal cords. Instead of the hollowed-out wood of the guitar, you have bones and cartilage in your face that surround air pockets. Once your vocal cords are set in motion, those air pockets vibrate in the Front Passage, and become the speakers of your voice. Because your facial bone structure is one-of-a-kind, so too is your voice one-of-a-kind.

The Cola Bottle

Another example of how the Front Passage works is to think of a cola bottle. The glass of the bottle is like the bones and cartilage of your face, and inside is the pocket of air.

What happens if you blow into the bottle? The air vibrates against the glass and sends out a rich tone. We will use that same concept to resonate your voice!

The Front Passage has cavities of air surrounded by bones and cartilage. They vibrate and act as the "speakers" of your voice.

GIVE IT A TRY!

QUICK RESONANCE EXERCISE – SENSATION OF VIBRATION

- Take a **Silent Breath** inhale with your tummy releasing OUT
- With your lips together but loose, bring your bellybutton IN
- Make the sound "Hmmmmm"
- Be aware of the **sensation of vibration** around your lips

WHAT ARE YOU AWARE OF?

Do you feel vibration in your lips and cheeks? The more it tickles your lips the better!

TRY IT AGAIN!

- Take a **Silent Breath** inhale with your tummy releasing OUT
- With your lips together but loose, bring your bellybutton IN
- Make the sound "Hmmmmm"
- Now "chew like a cow" while you say "Hmmmmm" – This makes sure your jaw and tongue are loose

HOME BASE

There's No Place Like Home

Let's take a leap to a new thought: Instead of thinking of the vocal cords in your throat as your instrument, let's *imagine* the Front Passage as *actually being your voice.* This new mental mapping will enable your voice to stay "out of your throat" and be vibrantly healthy. Think of the words you speak coming from your cheeks, as if your cheeks were your vocal speakers. Don't lift the pitch of your voice higher – just let the *vibration* of your words live in your cheeks. This is your new HOME BASE for both your speaking and singing voice.

> I call the Front Passage your "dominant resonator" or HOME BASE voice.

John's Voice
A Frog in His Throat

John was impressive. At only nineteen years old he was handsome, slim, 6'2", and had the most gorgeous high baritone trained voice I'd ever heard from a teen-ager. John was a local talent assisting me on my five-day singing intensive in Los Angeles. He was also signed up to participate in my workshop.

I was a bit puzzled. I had heard John sing magnificently with ease and confidence, and yet, as I chatted with him about the upcoming classes, it was like I was talking to a frog. All of his words came from his throat. I knew that if John kept it up, vocal damage would be next. I didn't mention anything to John as he was helping me get organized, but I had a plan to help him.

Twenty students sat in a huge half circle on the floor in front of me the first day of class. We had just conquered the first two elements of *The Revolutionary Send*, The Breath and Support, and now it was time to move on to Resonance. I turned to John on my right sitting on the floor at the end of the queue. "This one's for you." He listened intently.

With my instruction (and the students observing), John lifted the crackling sensation of the "frog in his throat" to a tickling vibration around his mouth and cheeks. With his words now sounding from the speakers of his cheeks, suddenly John's speech was clear and vibrant, just like his singing. And then something happened.

John started sobbing – and he couldn't stop.

> "This is great!" I exclaimed.
>
> "I'm embarrassed," John replied. His tears were uncontrollable.
>
> "You are releasing the emotions that were literally stuck in your throat! It's fantastic! Keep crying! What are you aware of?" John sobbed and sobbed. Then I saw a light bulb go off in his head.
>
> "I try to be perfect for my father." And there it was.
>
> "Don't clean up! Keep sobbing."
>
> "I can't really stop anyway." John's classmates were in awe. They all looked up to him as a mentor in the group – now they could be a support to him.
>
> "Good job, John!" a few of them shouted out. Others smiled and clapped for him. I kept up the positive vibes. This was a breakthrough!

"Who can lend John some sunglasses?"

"I can!" cried out one of students.

"Great! John, when you leave class today wear those sunglasses home and keep crying – that way you'll be covered even in public. Don't clean up!"

The next day, John shared with the class that he had sobbed a full twenty-four hours. They gave him a standing ovation! John felt relieved and joyous to have his voice clear. Even better, he was grateful to have a new awareness of his relationship with his father. Healing was on the way on every level.

DON'T LISTEN TO YOUR VOICE
Marilyn Horne

I love this quote from the great opera singer Marilyn Horne: "If your voice sounds good in your head, it's wrong! If your voice sounds bad in your head, it's right!"

Focusing on the *sensation of vibration* of your voice rather than on the *sound* of your voice will create natural overtones and vocal freedom.

In every note there are overtones – extra tones, also called frequencies, that we can't hear with our naked ear. A voice vibrating properly will generate these overtones which are stacked on top of the fundamental tone (the note we do hear) like a skyscraper: There's the fundamental frequency in the basement, and then the overtones ring on the lower floors, medium floors, and high above in the penthouse. Right now, we want these overtones to ring effortlessly.

Don't check the sound of your voice in your head. If you pull your voice back to listen to it in your own ear, it may seem like a big, round, deep sound in your head, but in reality, the sound out in the room is muffled. So, when the *sound* of your voice seems small and unappealing in your head, chances are it's beautiful in the room.

> *Do not focus on trying to hear the sound. You cannot hear your voice the way the audience hears your voice. Feel the vibration – don't listen to the sound.*

But don't worry! There is a way to listen to your voice in real time – How? *Sing in the shower!* You can hear your true timbre echoing back at you as the sound waves hit the tile walls. And if you can't always be taking a shower when you sing? Set a recording device while practicing and listen to your voice on the recording later. Just press play.

Sensation of Vibration
The Crystal Glass

When I was a kid, at Christmas time my mother would bring out the crystal stem-ware for our big holiday family gathering. We numbered about thirty and the kids ranged from the age of two to precocious thirteen. Sitting at the table waiting for dinner to arrive, the adults never seemed to be quiet, chattering over each other keeping a high decibel level of Christmas cheer.

My two big brothers had a trick they loved doing to get everybody's attention: They'd each put one hand at the bottom of a crystal glass to steady it, put water on the index and middle fingers, and then run their fingers around the lip of the glass. If done right, the crystal would send out a RINGGG into the room. The point was to get the *loudest* ring possible to be as *annoying* as possible!

I remember watching them hone their technique: They made sure not to have any haphazard napkins or flailing fingers touching the bell of the glass that would dampen the RINGGG that made the trick so fun and irritating. If the adults stopped all conversation and looked around like a fire alarm just went off, my brothers beamed with satisfaction!

As you discover the *sensation of the vibration* of your Resonance, you don't want any extraneous tension to dampen the potential of the overtones in your voice, like a pulled back tongue, or a tight jaw.

When working on the "Hmmmmm" exercise, make sure the tongue is relaxed: The tip of the tongue can rest on the back of your bottom teeth. The jaw is often a culprit of tension, so the chewing motion is a fantastic way to *release* the jaw. If the muscles are *moving,* it's not possible for them to clutch or hold tension*,* and more overtones will be free in your voice.

> *The reason opera singers don't need microphones to sing with an orchestra is because of the ringing overtones in their voices. The high overtone frequencies cut through the orchestra so even the audience in the back row balcony can hear the naked voice.*

My brothers' commitment was to make the RINGGG of the crystal glass as disruptive as possible at the Christmas party. For your voice, the commitment is to feel as much *sensation of vibration* as you can muster to let your gift LIVE in the most powerful and dynamic way possible.

HEALING VOCAL ISSUES
Habitual, Psychological, Physical

1. HABITUAL
Family Habits – How Do You Speak?

"*Singing is born out of speaking.*" If you can talk, you can sing. As children mastering language, we not only learn the formation of words, but we also learn where and how to resonate the voice from our family and community.

A variety of languages and accents resonate differently: French has more vowels that are nasal. German and Hebrew have more consonants spoken near or in the throat. Michigan natives speak with vowels that resonate piercingly nasal, while Australians speak with a fluid and fresh forward vibration.

Families can also pick up their own vibration. Michael Jackson's family members pitch their voices very high. Do you know a family where everybody speaks loudly? Softly? Monotone? Famous Broadway belter Ethel Merman had so much resonance in her voice that it seemed like she was always shouting. I wonder how her family spoke.

My job is to diagnose and guide each voice so that even with vocal habits, the speaking voice is free and healthy, and the singing voice is resonating in its full potential.

The most common vocal habit that seems to be in every community around the world is vocal fry. This habit of *speaking in the throat* is dangerous. With time, a polyp or nodule can form on the vocal cords – the dread of every singer, and the reason many a singing career can come to an end. Even worse, years later they might get what's called "vocal dysphonia" – a sort of freezing of the vocal cords, which not only stops the voice from working, but is downright painful.

And what I've discovered – vocal fry is contagious! No wonder it's prominent worldwide. I learned that firsthand.

The Yoga Center
Vocal Fry is Contagious

While visiting family in San Francisco, I went to a health center and signed up for a yoga class. There were two girlfriends in their twenties in front of me chit-chatting with the receptionist. One was a writer for the *San Francisco Chronicle* and the other a medical student. My sensitive ears immediately went to the Resonance of the voices of these young professionals — and let me tell you, my ears were shocked! Every word they spoke was in the throat. Their voices sounded coarse and gravelly, like rocks rubbing together. Even more shocking, when I started to speak to the receptionist, I was speaking the same way! *It was contagious!* Even though I knew perfectly well not to speak in my throat, I took on their vocal fry! Why would I do that? It dawned on me — perhaps because I was just visiting, I wanted to feel a part of the group. I wanted to belong. Those gals seemed "cool," and I wanted to be cool too!

Fortunately, I knew immediately how to remedy the situation. I got myself together. I switched my attention from the "I'm cool, I'm relaxed, I belong," mode with the bacon sizzling sound in my throat and directed my thoughts immediately to the Front Passage resonators. "Hmmmmm," I said under my breath. I brought the sensation of vibration right back to my lips and mouth.

That day I was the student! I had to walk the walk. I whispered silently to myself, "Speak through your cheeks, Mary — through your cheeks!"

2. PSYCHOLOGICAL

Kim Kardashian – Vocal Fry

Reality TV superstar Kim Kardashian (*Keeping Up with the Kardashians*) was perhaps the first to make vocal fry popular. I don't believe she does it consciously — but I do feel there is a psychological reason behind her vocal fry. When I hear Ms. Kardashian's throaty timbre, it says to me that she's subconsciously diminishing her power. Using vocal fry is a way to deflect her worldwide popularity — for being on a reality TV show — so that she can seem "normal" — as if to say to her viewers, "Ignore my fame, my fortune, my appeal. I'm really just like the rest of you."

What's truly remarkable is that after becoming a famous reality TV star, Kim Kardashian found another calling: studying law and helping with criminal justice reform. Ms. Kardashian worked tirelessly to advocate for a life sentence to be commuted of the nonviolent drug offender, Alice Johnson. As Ms. Kardashian spoke publicly and passionately about her work, something magical happened – her vocal fry disappeared. Why? When Kim Kardashian had a true passion – a commitment – something she believed in – something of value to share – her voice followed. Her speaking was powerful, vibrant, dynamic, and rich with resonant overtones. Ms. Kardashian didn't have to apologize for her fame. She found a purpose without judgment. It was a vocal triumph.

3. PHYSICAL

Pushing the Voice – Loud Restaurants

One of the biggest vocal dilemmas for all of us is being in loud restaurants and trying to speak above the noise and clatter to be heard. It's so easy to strain the vocal cords. Beware! When in loud establishments be sure to consciously engage your Super Bellybutton and use your cheeks as the speakers of your voice. If you do push your voice, stop talking, drink water, and get a good night's sleep. Repeat.

Beth
Cheerleading

My sister-in-law Beth has had a damaged voice since high school. She was an enthusiastic cheerleader and pushed her voice so much that she got nodules. It's a serious case – the doctor told Beth that the nodules on her vocal cords are like sandpaper. Not even an operation could remove the many course bumps on her vocal cords. The nodules are too small and there are too many of them.

Beth has had to manage with a rough voice her whole life. Her voice gets tired easily and friends and colleagues have such a hard time hearing her – especially on the telephone. It's also sad because Beth *loves* to sing, and she happens to be a talented musician. She is the only person I know who can hear a song once and remember every note and lyric.

Beth has since worked with me connecting her Breath and Support with her voice. Now when Beth focuses on placing her voice through her cheek resonators, her speaking voice is vibrant, and she can even sing! It's like the speakers of a stereo suddenly turning on. "I speak from my resonators!" Beth says proudly, and she sounds fantastic!

Beth will always have the sandpaper nodules on her vocal cords, but with her intention to connect her voice to her Resonance, Beth's voice is a miracle.

RESONANCE EXCERCISES

Connecting The Breath and Support with Your Voice

Now that you've learned about the first three important elements on the Voice Technique Side – **The Breath**, **Support**, and **Resonance** – it's time to connect them all together so you can always have healthy speaking and great singing.

LET'S PUT IT ON ITS FEET!

"Ssssss" EXERCISE

- Stand in front of a mirror
- Take a **Silent Breath** inhale – the tummy releases OUT
- Then swing the bellybutton IN on **"Ssssss"**
- Do that a few times

SAY "Hmmmmm"

- Again, take a **Silent Breath** inhale
- In the same manner that you bring the bellybutton IN with "Sssssss," now swing your bellybutton IN and say **"Hmmmmm"**

SAY "Hmmmmm" AND CHEW

- Again, say "Hmmmmm" and feel as much vibration as you can muster
- To release your tongue, rest the tip of the tongue on the back of your lower teeth
- Say "Hmmmmm," and chew like a cow

This exercise releases any jaw tension. FEEL the vibration. If your lips are tickling, that's perfect! Don't listen to the sound. Just focus on the sensation of the vibration around your lips saying "Hmmmmm."

You have just hooked up your **Breath** and **Support** with your voice —
Resonance!

WHAT ARE YOU AWARE OF?

Where do you feel the vibration? Is the vibration somewhere in the Front
Passage, like your mouth, lips, and cheeks? That's great! If you feel the vibration going into your throat, just redirect your intention for the vibration to ring
somewhere around and above your lips. Don't worry about the exact mechan-
ics of your throat, mouth, or jaw as you are chewing. Just chew. Being aware
of the sensation of vibration around and above your lips is enough. Your
intention to feel the vibration will direct your muscles to make the small
adjustments necessary.

SPEAKING EXERCISE

Now that you can feel the sensation of vibration around your lips and above, it's
time to connect it with speaking.

To identify the vowels and consonants, I will us the "International Phonetic Alphabet" (IPA) symbols. When I use the IPA, brackets will be used as follows:

[mi] as in "me"

[me] as in "may"

[ma] as in "ma"

[mo] as in "mow"

[mu] as in "moo"

GIVE IT A TRY!

SPEAKING – HANDS ON CHEEKS

- To start, put your hands ON your cheeks
- Take an easy inhale in the bottom of your lungs
- While bouncing your bellybutton IN, say **[mi]** and pull your hands AWAY from your cheeks
- Inhale – while bouncing the bellybutton IN, say **[me]** and pull your hands AWAY from your cheeks
- Inhale – while bouncing the bellybutton IN, say **[ma]** and pull your hands AWAY from your cheeks
- Inhale – while bouncing the bellybutton IN, say **[mo]** and pull your hands AWAY from your cheeks
- Inhale – while bouncing the bellybutton IN, say **[mu]** and pull your hands AWAY from your cheeks

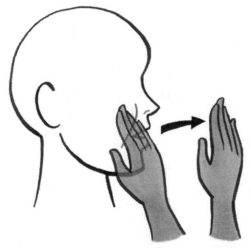

[m → i]
[m → ɛ]
[m → a]
[m → o]
[m → u]

SING

STACCATO EXERCISE – ADD PITCH

[mi ' me ' ma ' mo ' mu]

"Staccato" in Italian means "detached." Each syllable in a row will be detached and short. Let's do the same previous Speaking Exercise *with the hands* while adding PITCH to the spoken syllables and...voila! You're singing!

Choose a pitch that is around your speaking voice. The picture below shows the musical note middle C. For most, that's around your speaking voice. (For women and children, the middle C on the piano is the same pitch as your voice. For men, your voice will naturally sound an octave lower. For our purposes, I will call this note middle C for all.)

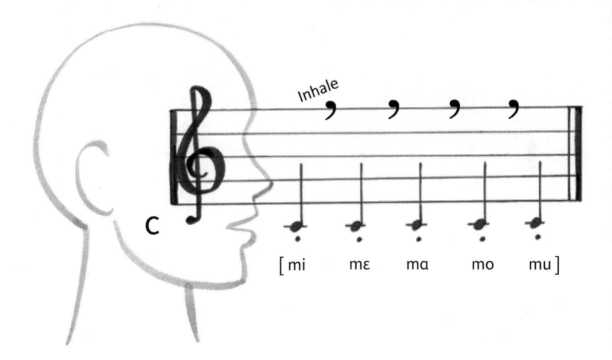

GIVE IT A TRY!

- Take a little inhale preparing for the first staccato (detached) note with your hands on your cheeks

- As the bellybutton bounces IN, add pitch to **[mi]** and pull your hands AWAY from your cheeks

- Inhale – As the bellybutton bounces IN, add pitch to **[me]** and pull your hands AWAY from your cheeks

- Inhale – As the bellybutton bounces IN, add pitch to **[ma]** and pull your hands AWAY from your cheeks

- Inhale – As the bellybutton bounces IN, add pitch to **[mo]** and pull your hands AWAY from your cheeks

- Inhale – As the bellybutton bounces IN, add pitch to **[mu]** and pull your hands AWAY from your cheeks

- Repeat the five vowels in a row, inhaling – then bouncing the bellybutton IN and pulling your hands AWAY from your cheeks for each syllable on pitch **[mi ' me ' ma ' mo ' mu]**

WHAT ARE YOU AWARE OF?

Can you feel vibration around your lips and cheeks? The hands pulling AWAY from the cheeks help you to adjust the vibration to ring in your Front Passage. Are you taking a little inhale and then bouncing the bellybutton IN for each syllable with pitch? Don't listen to the sound – just expect the feeling of a forward vibration as you speak each syllable with pitch. That is enough. Now you're singing!

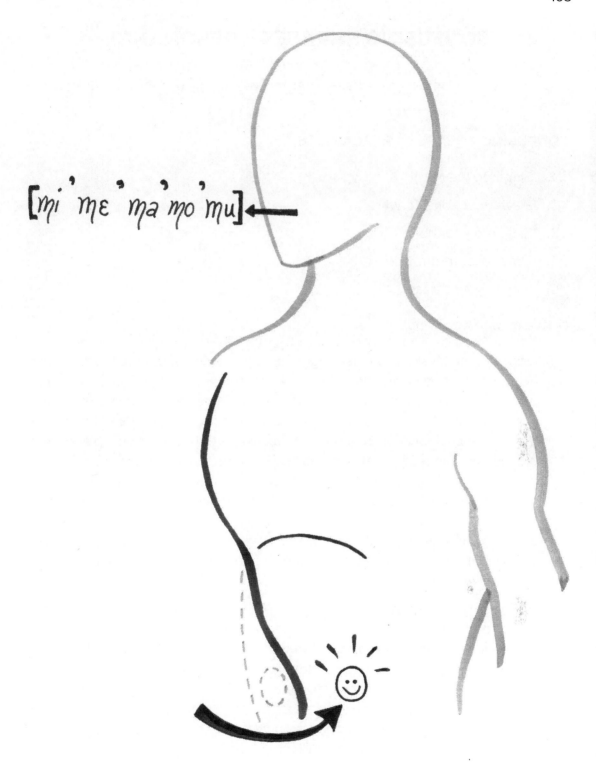

RESONANCE

CONFUSING PHRASES – RESONANCE

Let's revisit the *Confusing Phrases* from the beginning of the chapter and get them clear:

CONFUSING PHRASES – RESONANCE:

1. "Sing into the Mask"

2. "Place your voice forward"

3. "Sing into your nose"

4. "Open your throat"

5. "Sing in your throat"

Let's examine each one:

1. "Sing into the Mask." The Mask suggests singing into the front of the face: forehead, nose, cheeks, and lips. This is similar to my term, the Front Passage – but Mask implies a more specific front/forward location. "Sing into the Mask" can be an excellent command if the singer has been checking and listening to their voice back in their own ear. In this case, the focused front "placement" of the Mask can rectify that bad habit by bringing the Resonance forward. But if the natural position of the Resonance is already forward, the term Mask might push the voice too far forward and minimize the full vibration of the voice. My term the Front Passage is still forward, but it covers a larger area – from your upper lip and in front of your ears going straight up. The singer can enlarge their sounding board and amplify their voice to its maximum Resonance.

2. "Place your voice forward." For those like Beth who have nodules on their vocal cords, this command is an excellent cue to help resonate the voice. For those who sing in their throat or too far back in their head, I would also use this command. But for those who don't have these issues and sing beautifully in the Front Passage, I shy away from the word *Place* or *Placement*. For singers to *place* or *put* the voice in an *exact spot* can constrict the full potential of their voice. You want the Resonance to *live* and never to be *held*. I prefer to say, "Expect it there" rather than "Place it there."

> *It wasn't until I got the information about the Front Passage from my Master Voice Teacher Joan Heller that I understood my voice. One teacher had told me to "put" my voice way out front, while another had told me to "open" my voice. I always felt confused. Then, when I was told to think of my instrument as the Front Passage resonators, I suddenly felt a sense of security. I knew where my voice lived! It was a vibrant sensation that I could FEEL. Now I own my instrument! Powerful stuff.*

3. "Sing in your nose." Choosing to *place* the vibration only in your nose for most singers would make the sound pinched and nasal. That said, for someone who sings way back in the throat, "Sing in your nose" can actually correct the problem. The singer might feel like it's in the nose, but the adjustment brings the voice forward to engage the Front Passage resonators. In this case, believe it or not, the voice would be free and beautiful without a shred of nasality. For everybody else without this issue? Don't do it.

4. "Open your throat." The Home Base of the throat should be normal, just as if you were speaking. You don't speak with a wide-open throat, inducing a breathy sound, so don't do it when you're singing. However, there have been a few times when I've told a student to "Open your throat." The student was holding the throat so tightly that it needed to be released. In my experience, this sometimes could indicate that the student has been abused. The constricted throat acts as a kind of protection. In this case, opening and releasing the throat back to "normal" is essential for the sound and healing for the student. For those of you who are holding a very tight throat, the "Open your throat" command is helpful to bring the voice back to normal. However, for most of you, you don't have this issue, so please *do not open your throat*!

> *Think of the throat like a rubber band. When a rubber band has been stretched too far, it needs to come back to its closed, natural shape. When a rubber band is too tight, it needs to be stretched and released to its open natural shape.*

5. "Sing in your throat." The teachers who use this command want you to think of the vocal cords as your instrument. It is a fact that there *are* vocal cords vibrating and phonating in the throat. But if you *think* about your throat and vocal cords while singing, you invite unwanted tension and possible damage to the voice. Don't focus your mental attention on singing *in* the throat. There may be a moment in your creativity that you'll want an isolated sound to be "throaty." If you are making a conscious choice to have this sound on your artistic palate of vocal colors, then it may have a place in the world. Otherwise, NO.

Arianna
Capillary Fragility

A beautiful and talented young pop singer in Italy, Arianna, came to me while in the throes of a difficult diagnosis: Her doctor said she had very fragile vocal cords. The problem was related to *capillary fragility* – which meant that the capillary walls throughout her body were abnormally susceptible to rupture. Arianna's vocal cords were at high risk of hemorrhaging. To prevent this, the doctor suggested surgery.

I could tell that Arianna was worried about the surgery, but at the same time, I was alarmed when I heard her speaking in her throat – a severe case of vocal fry. After some investigation, I found out that Arianna was instructed to *make her vocal cords rub together* as a vocal exercise.

"This exercise is dangerous," I told her. "Nodules are little callouses that are formed by the friction of the vocal cords rubbing together. And in your case, your cords might even hemorrhage."

Arianna looked at me with tears welling up in her eyes. "I told my teacher it wasn't comfortable. I told her I didn't like it. She said not to worry – that it was completely healthy for my voice."

"Well, your doctor has detected *capillary fragility* and wants to do surgery to help you." Arianna nodded yes. "With your permission, let's practice some important voice techniques to take the pressure off your vocal cords so they can heal even before your surgery. Okay?"

"Okay," she smiled.

Fortunately, in just one lesson, Arianna realigned her thoughts to make her voice resonate in the Front Passage rather than in her throat. Along with connecting the proper Breath and Support (the other technique she studied never talked about Support), Arianna had fundamentally changed the way she sang.

Arianna had a choice – take a pass on the surgery and rely on the training, or do both. She decided to do both – help her vocal cords with a change in technique and have the operation.

Arianna told me that she applied all the techniques we did together. She's had a healthy voice ever since. Today Arianna is a successful professional singer.

Organize yourself... Please check off **Resonance**.

THE REVOLUTIONARY SEND

VOICE TECHNIQUE SIDE	EMOTIONAL LIFE SIDE
1. ~~The Breath~~	1. **Personalization**
2. ~~Support~~	2. **Fourth Wall**
3. ~~Resonance~~	3. **Sensory Condition**
4. **Floors**	4. **Need**
5. **Pyramid**	5. **Action**

You have now adjusted your *speaking* voice to be fresh and healthy for years to come with the first three elements of *The Revolutionary Send* – **The Breath, Support,** and **Resonance.** AND you've taken the first steps to SING with those three essential elements in place. Congratulations! That's a huge accomplishment already!

Before we discuss and sing with the last two elements on the **Voice Technique Side – Floors** and **Pyramid** – we need to jump across right away to the **Emotional Life Side** of *The Revolutionary Send,* starting with **Personalization**.

The BEST singing is not just about voice technique. The BEST singing is when the audience can connect to your emotional truth.

> **Your voice technique is in your emotions,
> and your emotions are in your voice technique.**

chapter four

PERSONALIZATION

BERNADETTE PETERS
Tell Me on a Sunday

I had just moved to New York to follow my dream to be on Broadway. I felt pretty isolated at the time – my family and friends were far away in California, and I was still getting over a guy. Well, what was there to get over? He had been my best friend in college, and we had done everything together, but romance was never in the picture. Never a kiss. He had given me a couple of signs that maybe that would change one day, but I had to come to terms with the fact that, well, he just wasn't that into me.

I decided to treat myself to a Broadway show. I had loved musicals my entire young life, but I'd never seen anything like this before: There was Bernadette Peters, completely alone on stage, sitting in the corner, reaching to the man she loved who was breaking up with her, crying her eyes out, and singing, "*Tell me on a Sunday, please.*" In the scene, the man was there with her – but this was a one-woman show, so there was no *real* man actually on the stage.

I didn't know what to call it at the time, but Bernadette Peters was in her Personalization singing directly to *her person*. She was so private, so vulnerable. She was exposing devastating pain as if nobody else was in the room, let alone a sold-out audience. Her excruciating loss of love hit my heart. Her voice was...perfect. There was no separation between sound and pain. If she didn't hit a note, I certainly wasn't aware of it. It was as if I were the only person in the theater, experiencing this intimate moment with her. I felt like she was singing just for me – understanding my painful truth: I'd never be with this man whom I loved. I sobbed my eyes out too.

PERSONALIZATION
1. Emotional Life Side

PERSONALIZATION – Make it Personal

The Goal: To make what you sing *personal* to you.

Why This Is Important: Linking *you* to your singing is the key that unlocks the interpretation of your songs and improves the sound of your voice in a way the technical components don't offer by themselves. When you merge what the songwriter wrote with your own life experience, your audience will hear it, feel it, and recognize their own personal story through your voice and song.

What Has To Change: You must stop trying to sound good. Don't close your eyes and sing to yourself, and don't put your hand over your ear to listen to your own voice. Instead, linking *you* to your song is the key.

MAKE IT PERSONAL

Let's talk about you. What's more personal than that?

The most important thing that sets you apart from all the rest is *you*.

> **You are enough. You're so enough. It's unbelievable how enough you are.**
> **– Susan Batson**

You are so interesting. That is the treasure. Your life, and the way you look at the world – the intimate relationships you have, or haven't had but wish you did – the times that brought you pure joy or made you feel worthless – all these are *your* goods, *your* truth, *your* assets. You are special just being you.

"If only I'd known my differentness would be an asset, then my earlier life would have been much easier." – Bette Midler

TWO WAYS TO PERSONALIZE
The Person and the Parallel Situation

There are two important Personalizations you will focus on:

1. The **Person** to whom you are singing

2. The **Parallel Situation** or event from *your* life that is similar to the story of the song you choose

1. THE PERSON

Whether you're singing publicly on a stage, or privately in your car, finding the person to whom you sing your song from your own life is so important. It brings a specificity of meaning to your song. The timbre of your voice finds a magical inflection that can't be taught technically. And on the other side – your voice technique improves when you sing to someone from your own life experience – from hitting high notes, to singing on pitch. As the student, and then the teacher, I have experienced both.

Mary, the Student
Hitting the High C through Personalization

I was auditioning for a review that celebrated the music of Andrew Lloyd Webber. I was given a variety of songs to sing for the audition. All was going quite well as I prepped the material – and then, snag! The high C at the end of "Think of Me" from *The Phantom of the Opera* freaked me out. I could usually sing that high C no problem, but all of a sudden, I was scared. Scared it wouldn't be there. Scared I'd screw it up in the audition. Worried it didn't sound good enough. I called upon my acting coach, Susan Batson.

Susan reminded me of Personalization. Instead of worrying about the note I had to hit at the end of the song, I picked the perfect person from my own life to sing the song to. As I sent my intimate story to *my* person, suddenly the high C was there every time, glittering, and effortless – even at the audition.

Mary, the Teacher
How Jason Sang on Pitch

I went to Los Angeles to teach a two-day singing workshop. I got very excited when one of the students told me he was an actor who had been in the movie *Rent*. A film actor who sings? Gold mine! Jason put the sheet music of a challenging pop song in front of me. I happily accompanied him on the piano.

Jason sang 100% of the notes off pitch.

Jason then shared with me that he hadn't sung in the movie, just acted – but he really wanted to sing. I believe everybody can sing, and on pitch, so we got to work. "This will be fun!" I assured Jason.

When working with a student who waivers off pitch, many voice teachers tell the student to focus on the pitch, *hear* it, and *change* it. In my experience, using only analytical thought to correct pitch doesn't work. The more the student *thinks* about the pitch, the more the pitch is wrong.

Putting the first three voice technique elements together – The Breath, Support, and Resonance was important – but the way to get Jason "pitch perfect" was all in his Personalization. Jason found *his* person to whom he was singing in the pop song. His story became so clear, so emotional, so precise. With the magical combination of voice technique and Personalization, Jason made the pop song his own.

At the end of the two-day workshop Jason sang 100% on pitch and made his classmates cry.

FIND THE PERSON FROM YOUR OWN LIFE
Who Would You Love to See Today?

Right now, **think of a person who you would love to see today**. When this person is far away, you miss them so much. It could be your grandmother, a long-lost friend, the love of your life, a dear one who has passed away, or even Sting.

GIVE IT A TRY!

PERSONALIZATION EXERCISE

Have some music nearby to turn on when I direct you to.

Please stand up with your eyes open or closed, as you like.

- Using your imagination, put the person who you'd love to see today directly in front of you
- As if the person was really there, put your hands on top of the head of the person and feel their hair
- Bring your hands to the forehead of the person and touch and feel the forehead
- Touch and feel the eyes of the person
- Feel the eyebrows
- Feel the nose of the person
- Feel the cheeks
- Feel the ears
- Feel the lips of the person
- Feel their chin
- Feel the jaw of the person
- Touch the neck of the person with your hands
- Feel their shoulders
- Bring your hands down the arms of the person
- Put their hands on top of your hands
- Now turn on the music
- As you hold the person's hands, move and dance with the person – you can have your eyes closed or open as you please

- Keep moving and dancing with the person
- Release sound as you dance with the person — say aaaaaah!
- Again, release sound as you dance with the person — say aaaaaah!

WHAT ARE YOU AWARE OF?

Do you feel a connection with the person? Are they more clear to you now? What did you feel when you released the sound? Do you feel emotional? What are those emotions? Don't clean up! Feel them all!

2. THE PARALLEL SITUATION

When you find a song you'd like to sing, ask yourself: why did I pick that particular song? Is there a certain message in the song that you can relate to? What do you remember from *your own life* that is similar to the story of the song? Did it recall a time you were unbelievably happy, or sad, or troubled? Think of all the details of that moment in your life. You are finding the Parallel Situation — the situation or event in the song that is parallel to your life.

This will help you find both the right person to sing the song to and to take the songwriter's experience and emotions of *their* event and personalize them to *your* situation. The audience will *feel* your truth. The listeners won't be thinking of your person or your Parallel Situation — Instead, they will be thinking of the person and situation in *their* lives and will be moved by your performance.

Finding the Parallel Situation
Falsettos

I had been cast as Trina in the musical *Falsettos* at the Charlotte Repertory Theater in North Carolina. Prepping for the role, I went to work in my acting class singing Trina's big Eleven O'clock Number, "Holding to the Ground."

My character, Trina

- was Jewish

- had been married to a closeted gay man who left her for another man

- had a thirteen-year-old child who needed to have his Bar Mitzvah

- and the only way to include all of the members of this modern family in the Bar Mitzvah was to hold the event in the hospital where her ex-husband's partner was dying from AIDS

During the song, Trina is alone on stage in the hospital explosively revealing her private pain of this complicated story. She sings over and over the lyrics:

> *But that's my life!*
> *Life is never what you planned,*
> *Life is moments you can't understand,*
> *But that's my life!*

I was in class belting out the song. I tried my hardest to use the Personalization. I knew how to sing loudly, and I had a fantastic sound — but nobody was moved by my performance. I wasn't in the truth of my character's devastating pain. How could I find a Parallel Situation? I'm not Jewish — I had never been married — I had never been left by a man for another man — I didn't have a child — No one who was close to me had ever died.

Then, a classmate screamed at me.

"Those things in your life that are all fucked-up — those are YOUR goods!" He beat his chest with passion. "It's YOUR life! Own that!"

My classmate was right. I did know that Trina's life was complicated and upside down — so I looked back on my own life to see if there was ever a time that I felt completely upside down. I found it. I had already explored the memory as an exercise in class a few weeks before.

I was thirteen years old sitting in my childhood bedroom by a large picture window. I could see a U-Haul truck in our driveway. Dad had just arrived to pick up his furniture. The divorce was final. I remembered watching Daddy steer the U-Haul up and out of the driveway – leaving me and our family behind.

Something clicked. Those horrible unspeakable feelings are the things that make me ME – Mary Setrakian. I had to tell MY story from the depths of my soul to connect to the real truth of Trina's story. The life of thirteen-year-old Mary was upside down. But that was my life.

I won the local critics award as Best Actress in a Musical for my performance as Trina in *Falsettos*.

As we move forward, please ruminate on *your* person from the Personalization Exercise. You can also brainstorm about different events in your life that you could use as your Parallel Situations to connect to your favorite songs (just like you do when you sing in your car when nobody can hear you). This is a wonderful opportunity to use sad and difficult moments in your life and make art out of them.

I promise you'll SING in the next chapter as you connect your Personalization to the second element on the Emotional Life Side of *The Revolutionary Send*, the **Fourth Wall.**

Organize yourself... Please check off **Personalization**.

THE REVOLUTIONARY SEND

VOICE TECHNIQUE SIDE	EMOTIONAL LIFE SIDE
1. The Breath	1. Personalization
2. Support	2. **Fourth Wall**
3. Resonance	3. **Sensory Condition**
4. **Floors**	4. **Need**
5. **Pyramid**	5. **Action**

Next up – **Fourth Wall**. When combined with **Personalization**, the **Fourth Wall** is the *key* to sing with your intimate vulnerability *in public*. Let's do this!

chapter five

FOURTH WALL

DANISH POP STAR TIM SCHŌU
Office Space

When Danish pop star Tim Schōu was recording his new album in New York, he sought me out for a lesson and some advice. He came to my studio, and we began with a chat. I asked Tim how things were going. He said he was writing and performing all over the place, and that producers worldwide were interested in his music. The bigwigs called him in for meetings where they'd interview him, and then hear him sing an original song or two – right in the office.

"And how is that going?"

"Good question."

"Do you always get a good response?"

"Sometimes I do. Sometimes...I'm not really sure."

I asked Tim to do a mock "meeting" for me right there. I played the producer and welcomed him to my office. Then I invited him to sing. Tim sat with his guitar, plucking at an introduction while looking at the floor. He seemed emotional, but I couldn't see his face. Tim started singing. *(Wow, what a gorgeous voice.)* There was an intense emotion in his sound, but Tim's eyes stayed closed for most of the song. I could see his cheeks getting all red, but I didn't feel anything. I just observed him. He ended the tune.

"You have an incredible depth, Tim, incredible...but you're hiding it."

"Yeah, I'm putting it off."

I was so taken by Tim's extraordinary sensitivity. For an artist, that is something to pray for, and Tim had it. But the tell-tale signs – looking down, closing his eyes – made it clear to me that Tim just needed a little clarity as to how to *share* his vulnerability, and not "put it off." Tim had to take the risk to expose his intimacy – a challenge on any day, but especially in a cold conference room with florescent lights, bad acoustics, and executives just two feet away. On top of all that, switching from a "meet and greet" with producers to an intense performance of an emotional song is really hard. It takes real tools to understand how to get there.

The answer? The Fourth Wall.

Tim had already chosen a person from his own life to sing to – he had written the song for a special lady. But now, he needed the Fourth Wall to create magic in the cold office space.

"After the 'meet and greet,'" I told Tim, "take a moment to set-up your song. Think of the woman you want to sing to. Create an imaginary wall between you and the producers sitting in front of you. Find a specific point on that Fourth Wall. In a meeting like that, it's perfect to put the person right between the heads of the executives. That way, you are not looking straight at them, which would make them extremely uncomfortable. Instead, they will see your eyes (*the eyes are the window to the soul*) and feel drawn into your story. See your lady's beautiful face right there on that wall. You will cocoon yourself in your privacy with her, and not let the executives make you feel self-conscious or embarrassed. You will literally *change the room* from a cold office space to your own intimate stage. The bigwigs will be flies on the wall, sharing your emotional experience."

After the lesson, Tim was off again to travel around the world. He notified me that he had yet another meeting with producers. The outcome this time? Success! They booked him.

FOURTH WALL

2. Emotional Life Side

FOURTH WALL – Focus & Singing Privately

The Goal: To place the imaginary Fourth Wall between you the singer, and the audience. You will find a point on the Fourth Wall and place your Personalization there. As you sing privately to your person, the audience will, at the same time, be able to share the intimacy you have created in your privacy.

Why This Is Important: It is one thing to sing in the shower, or in a car when no one is listening. But singing on a stage, or at a friend's wedding, or even for your family in the living room, can be downright scary. The more you look out at the audience, the more self-conscious, embarrassed, and nervous you might become. The Fourth Wall is a tool that will help you to focus on the story of your song and shut out those worries of judgment while you sing. The audience will fade away from your view so that you can be private with your person. The Fourth Wall helps you to "live" your vulnerable story rather than trying to make your voice sound "perfect." Singing a song is not about vocal perfection. Singing a song is about the journey.

What Has To Change: Instead of closing your eyes or aimlessly looking around the room as you sing, now you are going to use the Fourth Wall to "cocoon" yourself in your Personalization. Your audience will be like a fly on the wall, peering into your private world where they will be deeply moved by the intimate story you are telling.

WHAT IS THE FOURTH WALL?

The term Fourth Wall comes from stage acting. When you are standing on a stage looking out toward the audience, you have the wall behind you, the two wings to each side (which are the three walls), and then you have the Fourth Wall – the imaginary wall between you and the audience.

The Fourth Wall is the imaginary wall between the performer and the audience.

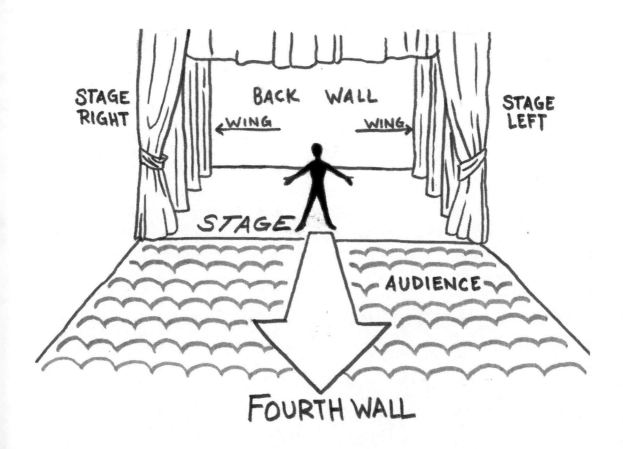

HOW TO USE THE FOURTH WALL
Making It Private

Wherever you are performing, be it on a Broadway stage or in your family's living room, you are facing the imaginary Fourth Wall. Pick a specific central point to anchor your Fourth Wall. In the theater, it might be an exit sign – at an outdoor rock concert, maybe a tree in the distance – at the family party, perhaps a painting on the wall behind your parents. In an audition, find a point between the heads of the casting directors at the table (like Tim did in his story), then place your Personalization on that point. (Later on, we will add other points on your Fourth Wall – right and left – but for now, you are only working on finding and using the central point.)

Please don't pick a point that's too high, too low, or off to the side – and be sure not to close your eyes. *The eyes are the window to your soul*, as the adage goes, and the audience needs to see your eyes in order to enter into your intimate story.

The Eyes Have It

I know, I know...when you close your eyes while you're singing you feel so much deep emotion. You feel the love! You feel the pain! You listen to your voice in your head and it sounds great. Well, here's the truth: When you close your eyes, perhaps *you* feel something deep and emotional, but the audience observes a self-indulgent performer listening to their own voice. Your voice may sound great in your head as you analyze your timbre and check the depth of your pain, but out in the audience we feel left out of the journey you're enjoying behind your shut eyes. *Open* your eyes, "see" your person, *send* your voice, and let everybody experience the connection of your emotions and free tone...not just you.

Breaking The Fourth Wall

Some songs call for singing *directly* to the audience. In this way you are doing what's called *breaking the Fourth Wall*. In a cabaret setting, I've been known to enter the stage from the back of the house (where the audience enters), singing directly to the crowd as I make my way to the stage. It's a fun surprise to literally make my audience a part of the show.

As performers, we can certainly get nervous even chatting or singing directly to audience members. A fun Personalization when breaking the Fourth Wall is to "put a person in the audience" who thinks you are a superstar – somebody who thinks you have it all. You're funny! You're gorgeous! You're magnificent! The positive essence of that special person in your audience will give you a little extra courage to welcome your patrons and look 'em in the eye. Those strangers will become your newfound friends, and you'll have them in the palm of your hand.

But more often than not, you must sing a song as if you are alone on stage with the audience peering into your private world.

Lee's Lover
If Your Personalization is in the Audience

You might wonder – if the person you are using as your Personalization is in the audience (and you're singing a song as if you are alone with that person), should you sing directly to them? That's what my student Lee did at a Singing Showcase off-Broadway. Because Lee's new boyfriend was in the audience, he went rogue from my Fourth Wall direction. Let me tell you, Lee's vocals are always off-the-charts magical, and this time was no different as he sang a Marvin Gaye love ballad. Gorgeous! Lee looked directly at his lover in the sixth row and sang the entire song – only to him. At the end of the show, a young woman came running up to Lee with tears in her eyes. "Your voice is incredible! So incredible! But I wanted you to sing to ME! Why didn't you sing to MEEEEE?!" As I overheard the young lady's plea, I chuckled to myself and whispered under my breath – *Fourth Wall*. If Lee had put the image of his lover on the center point of his imaginary Fourth Wall and had sung to him there, rather than directly to him in the audience, *everybody* in the audience (including his lover *and* the young woman) would have felt like Lee was singing only to them.

PERSONALIZATION AND FOURTH WALL EXERCISES

Whether you're singing for your mom in the kitchen, or you're performing at a stadium with thirty thousand people watching you, here are the tools to set-up your Personalization and Fourth Wall.

PERSONALIZATION

Earlier, you personalized to whom you are singing: the person you'd love to see today. Let's say that this person is far away from you now, and you miss them so much. Think of that person, and answer these questions to yourself about them:

What is the strongest physical feature of the person?

Be specific: Are the eyes the strongest physical feature of the person? The face? Maybe the strongest feature is their hair, nose, or shoulders? Are they tall?

What is the strongest human quality of this person?

Is this person funny? Sincere? Generous? Brash? Aloof? Gentle? Excellent! You're ready!

Now let's go through the exact steps of how to set-up your Fourth Wall with your Personalization – and SING. I have picked my father, so I'll use my preparation as an example. This exercise connects all the elements we've covered so far: **The Breath**, **Support**, **Resonance**, **Personalization**, and **Fourth Wall.**

SETTING UP YOUR PERSONALIZATION AND FOURTH WALL

1. Wherever you are right now, stand up, and find a central point in front of you on your Fourth Wall. What do you see? Maybe a lampshade, a window, a tree, a houseplant.

   – When I stand up, directly in front of me I see a painting on the wall, so I'll make the painting my object on my Fourth Wall.

2. Think of the person you would love to see today. This person is far away from you, and you miss them so much. What is the strongest physical feature of your person and the strongest human quality? See the person on your Fourth Wall on the object you have chosen.

   – I'd love to see my father today. My father has passed away, so yes, I miss him so much. My father's strongest physical feature is his face, and

> *his strongest human quality is his generosity. I see his face on the central point I've chosen – the painting on my Fourth Wall – and I can feel his generosity.*

3. If your person "disappears" on your Fourth Wall, just bring the strongest physical feature and human quality of your person back to your center point. You won't actually "see" the person in front of you. The theatrical "seeing" is, at times, just a feeling in the body.

   – If my father disappears, I just bring his face back in front of me on the center point of my Fourth Wall. Using my imagination, I can theatrically "see" my father in front of me and feel his generosity.

ADDING PERSONALIZATION AND FOURTH WALL TO THE VOCAL EXERCISES

Now with your **Personalization** set-up on your **Fourth Wall**, let's go to our vocal exercises and connect the voice technique elements we've done so far: **The Breath, Support,** and **Resonance.**

Our voice technique is rather like a Domino Effect – we must have the first two elements, **The Breath** and **Support** hooked up correctly, or none of the other elements that follow will be successful – so let's do a quick review.

My favorite exercise to hook up **The Breath** and **Support** is one you know from the Support chapter – the "Ssssss" Exercise.

"Ssssss" EXERCISE

- Stand in front of a mirror

- Take an easy inhale and see your tummy release OUT in the mirror

- As you exhale, SWING the bellybutton IN and say "Ssssss"

- Watch your sternum in the mirror freely bounce OUT as you swing the bellybutton IN – This means you are in the hook up of **The Breath** and **Support**

- Repeat as much as you like

- Inhale – exhale "Ssssss" – inhale – exhale "Ssssss" – inhale – exhale "Ssssss"…

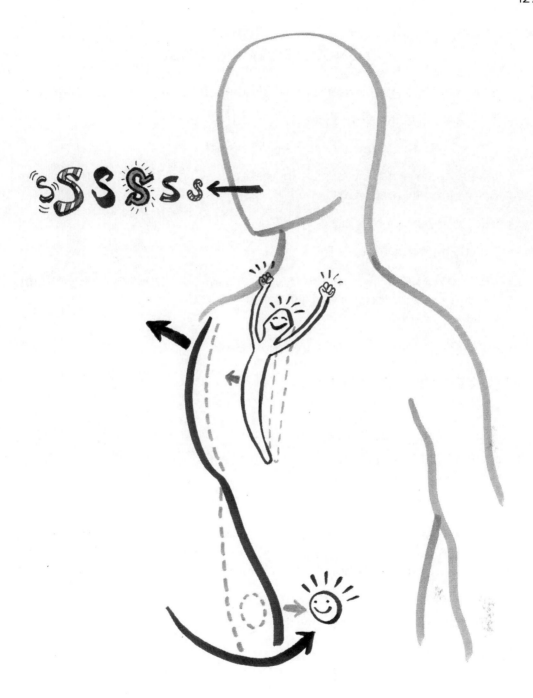

It's my intention to have everybody in the world practicing "Ssssss" every day so that their Breath and Support are honed for healthy speaking and singing! (Please join my movement!)

Now with **The Breath** and **Support** hooked up and ready to go, let's connect them with **Personalization** and **Fourth Wall** using the Tongue Trill and Lip Trill Exercises as the **Resonance**.

FOURTH WALL

TONGUE TRILL EXERCISE

- See your **Personalization** on the central point of your **Fourth Wall**

- Take an easy inhale, **The Breath**

- SWING the bellybutton IN and say **"Ssssss"**

- Inhale again – as you exhale instead of saying "Ssssss," you scoop the bellybutton IN and say **"Drrrrr"**

- **SEE** your person on your Fourth Wall

- **SEND** them the Tongue Trill

- Really have fun here – Your person is far away, and you want to see them – Send them the Tongue Trill as if you were saying, "HELLO!" – You can even wave at them

- "Drrrrr" – inhale – "Drrrrr" – inhale – "Drrrrr"

WHAT ARE YOU AWARE OF?

Did you see your person? Did they receive your Tongue Trill? Did you have fun saying "HELLO!?" Do you feel emotional seeing the person you miss? Don't clean up! Feel it all. Bravo!

LIP TRILL EXERCISE

Just like the Tongue Trill, now let's connect the Lip Trill to the same exercise:

- See your **Personalization** on the central point of your **Fourth Wall**

- Take an easy inhale, **The Breath**

- SWING the bellybutton IN and say **"Ssssss"**

- Inhale again, as you exhale instead of saying "Ssssss," you scoop the belly-button IN and say **"Brrrrr"**

- **SEE** your person on your Fourth Wall

- **SEND** them the Lip Trill

- If you're having trouble with the lips trilling, take your two index fingers and push UP your cheeks adjacent to the corners of your mouth – try again

- Have fun – Remember, your person is far away, and you miss them so much – Send them the Lip Trill and say, "HELLO!" – You can wave at them, "HELLO!"

- "Brrrrr" – inhale – "Brrrrr" – inhale – "Brrrrr"

NOW BEND YOUR KNEES AND RELEASE YOUR HEAD

- As your bellybutton moves IN and you say "Brrrrr," bend your knees to feel the Bellybutton-Down Support

- At the same time nod your head "yes" – let your head release as you say...

- "Brrrrr" – inhale – "Brrrrr" – inhale – "Brrrrr"

WHAT ARE YOU AWARE OF?

Did you see your person? Did they receive your Lip Trill? Were you able to bend your knees and release your head? If your lips were moving, you were in the correct Support and full release. Do you miss your person? Bravo!

STACCATO EXERCISE

[mi ' me ' ma ' mo ' mu]

Now let's put all the same elements together as you sing the Staccato Exercise. Choose a pitch that is around your speaking voice. (In the illustration I've noted middle C. If it's too high or too low for you, just change the pitch to where it's comfortable for you around your natural speaking voice.)

> **Reminder: For women and children, the middle C on the piano is the same pitch as your voice. For men, your voice will naturally sound an octave lower. For our purposes, I will call this note middle C for all.**

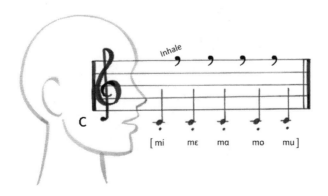

FOURTH WALL

GIVE IT A TRY!

- See your **Personalization** on the central point of your **Fourth Wall**
- Take a little inhale in between each staccato note – the tummy releases OUT
- As you exhale, the bellybutton bounces IN with each staccato syllable
- Feel a vibrant [m] on your lips with each syllable
- Send the Staccato Exercise to your person

[mi] – inhale – **[me]** – inhale – **[ma]** – inhale – **[mo]** – inhale – **[mu]**

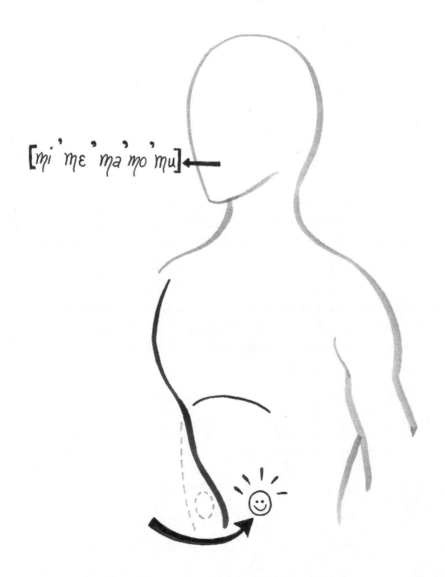

SING

Now let's do the same exercise, but instead of staccato short notes with a breath in between each syllable, you will do the Legato Exercise.

LEGATO EXERCISE

"Legato" in Italian means "tied together" – so musically you will sing all of the same syllables in a row but connecting them as smoothly as possible one to the next, all in one breath. [mi – me – ma – mo – mu]

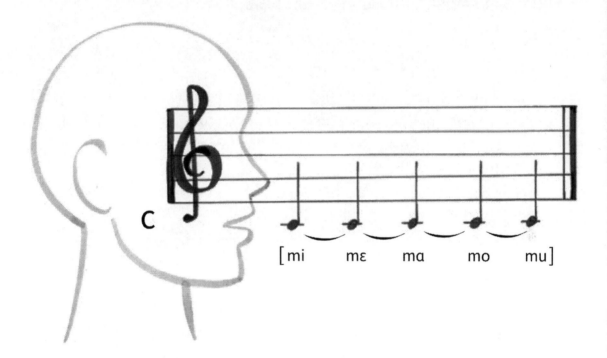

[mi   mɛ   mɑ   mo   mu]

GIVE IT A TRY!

SAY "Hmmmmm" AND CHEW

- See your person on the object you've chosen on your **Fourth Wall**
- Take an easy **Silent Breath** – the tummy releases OUT on the inhale
- Initiate the **Support** from your bellybutton – moving IN
- **Say "Hmmmmm"** – Feel the **Resonance** around your mouth and **CHEW**

WHAT ARE YOU AWARE OF?

Do you feel the [m] vibration around your mouth when you say "Hmmmmm" and chew? (Don't open your throat and let it fall into the back. Expect the vibration only in the FRONT.) How does it feel when you say "Hmmmmm" and chew? The jaw movement releases any tension you might have in your mouth, and you'll feel even more vibration. Do you feel more vibration? That's what you want – as much *sensation of vibration* as you can muster!

LEGATO EXERCISE [mi – me – ma – mo – mu]

- See your person on your **Fourth Wall**

- Take an easy **Silent Breath** through your nose and mouth at the same time

- Initiate the **Support** from your bellybutton – moving IN

- As your bellybutton moves IN, SEND out the syllables connecting smoothly in a row through the [m] **Resonance** you felt when you said "Hmmmmm" **[mi – me – ma – mo – mu]**

- Bring your arm up slowly and **REACH** to your person as you sing the exercise **[mi – me – ma – mo – mu]**

- Repeat: As you REACH to your person, relax your tongue so the tip of the tongue touches your bottom teeth, and move and your jaw side to side as you sing **[mi – me – ma – mo – mu]**

- Feel the vibration in your **Front Passage Resonators** around your mouth as you SEND the Legato Exercise to your person, moving your jaw side to side

WHAT ARE YOU AWARE OF?

Could you see your person? Did they receive the Legato Exercise? Did you REACH to your person? Did you relax your tongue and release your jaw moving it side to side? Did any emotions come up? If so, don't clean up! Let the emotions live, even in the exercises.

HAPPY BIRTHDAY

Now you're ready to sing a song to try out the concept for yourself – "Happy Birthday." You may be wondering, why is Mary introducing such a simple song for these exercises? For me, it's so helpful that you already know "Happy Birthday." That allows us to focus solely on technique. Plus, moving forward, we're going to connect all of the remaining *Revolutionary Send* elements, both technical and emotional, to the same song. And then – SPOILER ALERT! – in the final chapter of our ten elements, we'll visit the iconic version, *Happy Birthday Mr. President*, sung by the 1960's sex symbol, Marilyn Monroe. You'll get to hone *your* iconic version a la Marilyn. So, stay with me here as we connect "Happy Birthday" to your **Fourth Wall**.

HAPPY BIRTHDAY – EXERCISE

You are going to sing *just the first line* of "Happy Birthday" to your person who is far away from you. You miss them so much, and it's their birthday. Here is the first line:

Happy birthday to you, (inhale) **Happy birthday to you**

You will sing "Happy Birthday" around the natural pitch of your speaking voice. Don't try to sing higher, and don't try to sing lower – just easy from around the same pitch where your speaking voice lives. For most of us, that's near middle C, so here are the notes written around middle C.

Once again, let's use the tools you've learned so far to SING to the person who you'd love to see today. Those tools are: **The Breath, Support**, and **Resonance** connecting to your **Personalization** and **Fourth Wall**.

GIVE IT A TRY!

The person who you'd love to see today is now far away from you. You miss them so much, and it's their birthday. Put your **Personalization** on the object that you chose on your **Fourth Wall**. What is their strongest physical feature and their strongest human quality? See your person there.

SAY "Hmmmmm" AND CHEW

1. Take an easy **Silent Breath** through your nose and mouth at the same time

2. Initiate the **Support** from your bellybutton – moving IN

3. **Say "Hmmmmm"** – Feel the **Resonance** around your mouth and **CHEW**

SPEAK THE WORDS

4. Again, take an easy **Silent Breath** through your nose and mouth

5. Initiate the **Support** from your bellybutton – moving IN

6. **Now just SPEAK** the words to your person from the **Resonance** you felt around your mouth when you said, "Hmmmmm"

7. **Happy birthday to you,** (inhale) **Happy birthday to you**

SING HAPPY BIRTHDAY

8. See your person on your **Fourth Wall**

9. Take an easy **Silent Breath** – the tummy releases OUT

10. Initiate the exhale **Support** from your bellybutton – moving IN

11. **SEND and SING** the first two lines of HAPPY BIRTHDAY to the person you'd   love to see today and who you miss so much

12. Repeat as much as you like

Happy birthday to you, (inhale) **Happy birthday to you**

WHAT ARE YOU AWARE OF?

Did you see your person on your Fourth Wall? Did you send the song to your person? What did you feel? Did you feel the sensation of missing your person? If your eyes were open and you saw the person on your Fourth Wall, then the audience could enter into your story, even when singing a simple song like "Happy Birthday." *The eyes are the window to the soul.*

You just connected **The Breath, Support**, and **Resonance** with your **Personalization** and **Fourth Wall**! This is the first step towards using these elements all together. Great work!

Organize yourself... Please check off **Fourth Wall**.

THE REVOLUTIONARY SEND	
VOICE TECHNIQUE SIDE	**EMOTIONAL LIFE SIDE**
1. ~~The Breath~~	1. ~~Personalization~~
2. ~~Support~~	2. ~~Fourth Wall~~
3. ~~Resonance~~	3. **Sensory Condition**
4. **Floors**	4. **Need**
5. **Pyramid**	5. **Action**

With **Personalization** and the **Fourth Wall** ready to go, let's head back to finish up the last two elements on the **Voice Technique Side** – **Floors** and **Pyramid**. These two elements work together with your **Resonance** to find your true range and hit the high notes with ease. Let's first take a deep dive into what the **Floors** are and then put it all together with the **Pyramid.** Ready? Here we go!

chapter six

FLOORS

JAMES GANDOLFINI

I've got to tell you...
I always feel so much better when I leave here

"James! You just sang a high G like James Brown. That was fantastic!" "I'm glad *you* think so."

The late great *Sopranos* star, James Gandolfini, came to my studio three times a week as he was preparing for his singing-debut role in John Turturro's film, *Romance & Cigarettes*. Actually, he wasn't supposed to sing in the movie – only lip sync to the likes of Bruce Springsteen, Engelbert Humperdinck, and James Brown. In any case, James wanted to sing. We had to get James' voice to resonate beautifully throughout his entire range – both the low notes and the high notes. James was ready for the Floors.

Low notes can be deceiving. They seem like they'll be easy. But when James sang in his "easy" low range, his voice moved into his nose, and his tones sounded nasal. I instructed James to *feel* the vibration on the lowest floor of the Front Passage – around his mouth. When James felt the vibration on his lips and widened the vibration into his cheeks instead of pushing it higher into his nose, suddenly his voice was his own – rich, vibrant, balanced, easy. No more nasality.

But James had to sing high notes too. I instructed him to find a higher floor around his forehead when he sang the last note of his song. James belted it out, *Lonely is a man – withoooooout looooooove!* He couldn't even believe he was hitting those notes. He never complimented himself, but I sure did! "That's it!"

It's scary to sing publicly for the first time. After working with me for several weeks, James took the risk to sing through the Floors of his range every time — and he did it perfectly.

The last day of our lessons, James sat on my couch reflecting, "I've got to tell you...I always feel so much better when I leave here." He was ready. Director John Turturro decided to use James' voice in the movie instead of just lip-syncing along with the soundtrack. He was that good.

FLOORS

4. Voice Technique Side

FLOORS – Your Range

The Goal: To discover your range, you will integrate the **Floors** into your voice technique.

Why This Is Important: To sing in your full range from low notes to high notes is not just about being inspired. There is a technique that applies the physics of singing. In my method, **Resonance**, **Floors**, and **Pyramid** are the tools. You already know about **Resonance**. Learning about the **Floors** is the next step to this information. (Then comes **Pyramid**.)

What Has To Change: You will now layer the image of the **Floors** on top of your Front Passage **Resonance**. The **Floors** will be your guide as you sing up and down the scale.

"What have you been taught or heard about increasing your range?"

That's the next question I ask first time students. Here are some of their responses.

CONFUSING PHRASES – FLOORS:

1. "Listen to the pitches as you go up the scale"
2. "Sing as if you are yawning"
3. "Push your voice down for low notes"
4. "Strengthen your vocal cords"

We will revisit these *Confusing Phrases* at the end of the chapter. First, let's learn about the Floors and how to discover your true vocal range.

As we contemplate the task of going *up and down the scale*, let's remember for a moment the Home Base *dominant resonator* from Chapter Three on **Resonance — The Front Passage**.

THE FRONT PASSAGE

Reminder: The Front Passage is the area in your face located from your upper lip and in front of your ears going straight up. This "passage" in your head is like the sounding board in a piano. The Front Passage houses the resonators or "speakers" of your voice. The bones and cartilage in the Front Passage surround cavities of air. These air pockets vibrate against the shape of your bones and cartilage, resonating the signature sound of *your* voice.

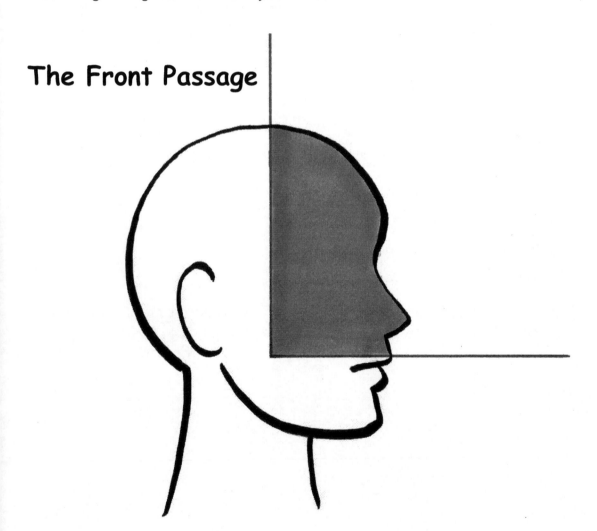

The Front Passage

Now, we layer *on top* of the Front Passage the image of the FLOORS.

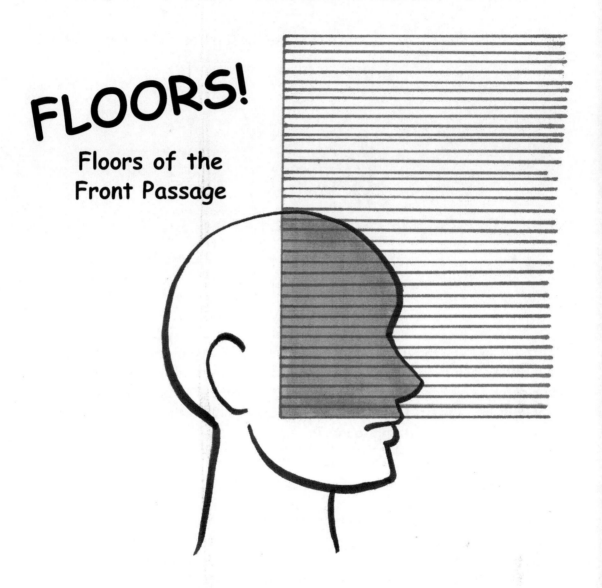

As you sing *up and down the scale*, you'll be guiding your voice up and down the **FLOORS of the Front Passage.**

Up the Scale – Up the FLOORS of the Front Passage

It is quite simple to go *up the scale*: Just as a pianist guides their fingers up the keyboard of a piano, or a violinist and guitarist guide their fingers up the neck of their instruments for the higher notes – as you *sing up the scale*, you are going to guide your voice up the **Floors of your Front Passage.**

THE FRONT PASSAGE WITH THE MUSICAL STAFF

In the illustration below, you can see the notes on the treble clef staff adjacent to the face.

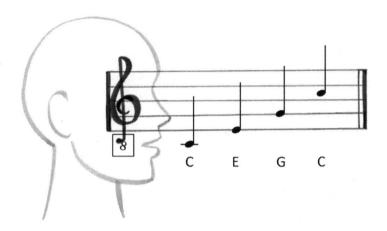

> **For the men, remember that your voice will naturally sound an octave lower than the written notes. From now on and for our purposes, I will use the treble clef for all exercises, but indicate with the <u>number 8</u> below the treble clef (highlighted in the box) that the men's voices will naturally sound one octave below of what is written in the music.**

THE LOWEST FLOOR – Around Your Mouth, Middle C and Below

The mouth is the lowest floor of the Front Passage. You already know to expect middle C and your speaking voice to live around your mouth. Even for the notes that go below middle C, you will think of the lowest floor at your mouth. *Don't push down* to sing those lower notes. Keep the *sensation of vibration* at your mouth.

UP THE SCALE – UP THE FLOORS

You can see in the illustration above that as you go up the scale, each note on the staff lives on a higher floor in the Front Passage. For example, the note E lives around the upper lip, the note G lives around the cheek area, and the C above middle C lives around the eyes.

You might wonder, would an extremely high voice or an extremely low voice also fit this example? The short answer is "yes, it's close enough." Trust that your voice will ring somewhere "around" the floors I give you. It will serve you well!

SLIDING EXERCISES UP AND DOWN THE FLOORS

Sliding Hum Exercise – "Hmmmmm"

Let's start with saying "Hmmmmm" to get acquainted with the **Floors** – Sliding Up and Down the Floors of the Front Passage.

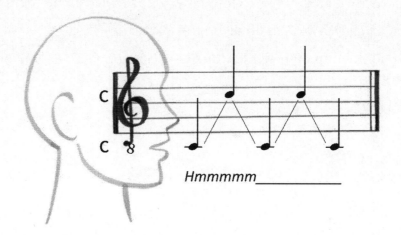

Hmmmmm_____

In the picture above, I've indicated sliding your voice up and down an **octave interval** – from middle C to the C above. An **octave interval** is the distance of 8-tones between two pitches. Think of the first word "Somewhere" from that famous song from *The Wizard of Oz*: "Over the Rainbow"

Sing it to yourself now:

Somewhere over the rainbow...
"Some – where" = an octave interval

Now you'll be *sliding* your voice on the "Hmmmmm" Exercise from middle C to the octave C above. Like before, you don't have to sing the exact C pitches – You can choose whatever octave leap is comfortable for you in your range. Be aware that as you slide your voice up and down the octave interval on "Hmmmmm," you'll be guiding the [m] vibration (like humming) *straight up and down* the **Floors** of your Front Passage from your *mouth up to around your eyes, and back down.*

GIVE IT A TRY!

START WITH THE "Ssssss" IN THE MIRROR TO MAKE SURE THE BREATH AND SUPPORT ARE IN PLACE

- Stand in front of a mirror
- Take an easy inhale – see your tummy release OUT in the mirror
- As you exhale, SWING the bellybutton IN and say "Ssssss"
- Watch your sternum in the mirror freely bounce OUT as you swing the bellybutton IN
- Repeat

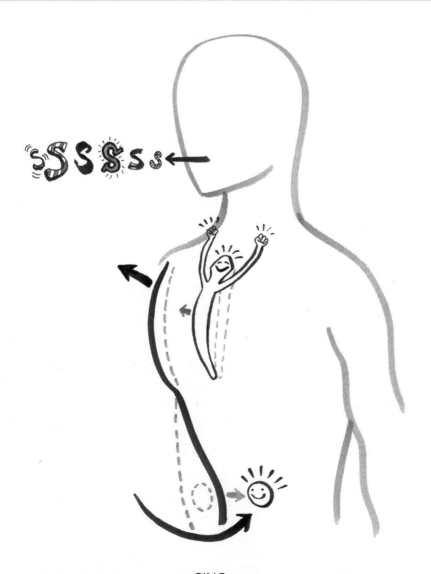

SING

SLIDING UP AND DOWN THE FLOORS IN AN OCTAVE – "Hmmmmm"

- Think of your **Personalization** – the person who you'd love to see today – they are far away from you, and you miss them so much

- Stand and put your **Personalization** on your **Fourth Wall**

- Take a **Silent Breath** inhale – your tummy releases OUT

- As the bellybutton **Support** swings IN, slide your voice in an octave straight up and down through the **Floors** of your Front Passage on **"Hmmmmm"** and chew

- The bellybutton moving IN is *leading* the humming vibration

- Feel the *sensation of vibration* at your mouth and sliding up to around your eyes as you guide your voice up and down the octave interval and chew

WHAT ARE YOU AWARE OF?

Can you *feel* the vibration of [m] going up and down the **Floors** of your Front Passage? Chewing releases tension in your jaw, so you feel even more vibration as you slide your voice on "Hmmmmm." Don't let the vibration fall back in your throat. Guide the [m] vibration straight UP and DOWN the **Floors** of the Front Passage. You are not going super high right now – just an octave leap (like the octave interval in *Some – where)*. As you chew, keep discovering the *sensation of vibration* from your mouth up to around your eyes. Be aware of your bellybutton vibrantly moving in and *leading* the [m] vibration up and down the **Floors**.

Sliding Tongue Trill Exercise – "Drrrrr"

Let's use the **Tongue Trill Exercise** to get acquainted with **Floors**.

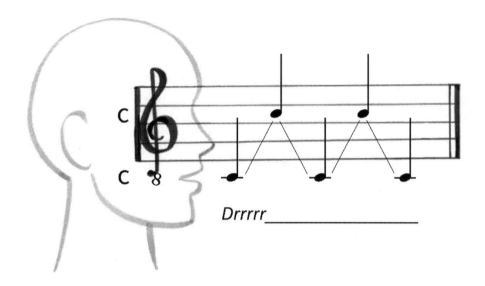

*Drrrrr*_____

GIVE IT A TRY!

START WITH THE "Ssssss" IN THE MIRROR

- Stand in front of a mirror
- Take an easy inhale – see your tummy release OUT in the mirror
- As you exhale, SWING the bellybutton IN and say "Ssssss"
- Watch your sternum in the mirror freely bounce OUT as you swing the bellybutton IN
- Repeat

SLIDING UP AND DOWN THE FLOORS IN AN OCTAVE – "Drrrrr"

- See your **Personalization** on your **Fourth Wall**
- Take a **Silent Breath** inhale – your tummy releases OUT

- As the bellybutton **Support** swings IN, send out a Tongue Trill – "Drrrrr" to your person
- Slide the Tongue Trill in an octave straight UP and DOWN the **Floors** of your Front Passage from your mouth up to around your eyes
- As you Tongue Trill up and down the scale, be aware of the Super Bellybutton swinging IN *leading* your trilling tongue
- Feel the *sensation of vibration* up and down the **Floors** of your Front Passage

WHAT ARE YOU AWARE OF?

Is your tongue trilling "Drrrrr"? Can you *feel* the trilling vibration going up and down the **Floors** of your Front Passage? Keep discovering the *sensation of vibration* sliding "Drrrrr" in an octave interval from your mouth to up around your eyes. Be aware of your bellybutton vibrantly swinging IN and *leading* the Tongue Trill.

Sliding Lip Trill Exercise – "Brrrrr"

Now let's do the same exercise but with the Lip Trill!

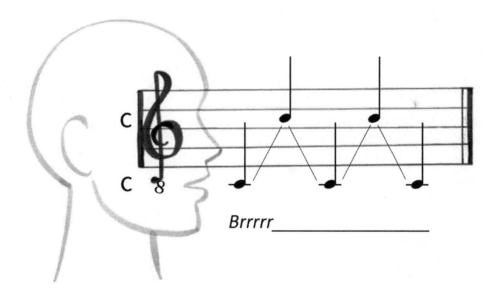

*Brrrrr*_____

GIVE IT A TRY!

START WITH THE "Ssssss" IN THE MIRROR

- Stand in front of a mirror

- Take an easy inhale – see your tummy release OUT in the mirror

- As you exhale, SWING the bellybutton IN and say "Ssssss"

- Watch your sternum in the mirror freely bounce OUT as you swing the bellybutton IN

- Repeat

SLIDING UP AND DOWN THE FLOORS IN AN OCTAVE – "Brrrrr"

- Stand and put your **Personalization** on your **Fourth Wall**

- Take a **Silent Breath** inhale – your tummy releases OUT

- As the bellybutton **Support** swings IN, send out a Lip Trill – "Brrrrr" to your person

- Slide the Lip Trill in an octave interval straight UP and DOWN the **Floors** of your Front Passage *expecting* the **Resonance** to vibrate from your mouth up to around your eyes

- If you're having trouble with the lips trilling, take your two index fingers and push UP your cheeks adjacent to the corners of your mouth – try again

- Feel the *sensation of vibration* through the **Floors**

WHAT ARE YOU AWARE OF?

Are your lips trilling "Brrrrr"? If not, with your index fingers push up your cheeks adjacent to the corners of your mouth to make your lips more fleshy. Can you *feel* the trilling vibration going up and down the **Floors** of your Front Passage? Keep discovering the *sensation of vibration* sliding "Brrrrr" in an octave interval from around your mouth to up around your eyes. Be aware of your bellybutton vibrantly swinging IN and *leading* the Lip Trill.

Sliding up and down the Floors of the Front Passage is like a guitarist moving their fingers up and down the frets of their guitar for the lower and higher notes.

HAPPY BIRTHDAY – ADDING THE FLOORS

Now let's revisit "Happy Birthday." You've already sung the **first line** of the song. Here it is again!

I've put the face in the staff to remind you where the melody of "Happy Birthday" lives on the **Floors** as you sing the song.

- The first phrase – ***Happy birthday to you***, will live around your mouth and upper lip

- The second phrase – ***Happy birthday to you***, will start at your mouth and then move up to your cheeks when you sing "to you"

GIVE IT A TRY!

- Think of the person who you'd love to see today – you miss them so much and it's their birthday

- Put your **Personalization** on the center point of your **Fourth Wall**

- Take an easy inhale – **The Breath**

- As you swing your bellybutton **Support** IN, sing to your person *Happy birthday to you, Happy birthday to you*

- Be aware of the **Floors** from your mouth up to around your cheeks as you sing *Happy birthday to you*

Diction Trap – "Birthday"

Before we venture ahead singing this octave interval, we *first* must look at a diction trap for the word "birthday" that has caught many a singer off guard – Singing an American [r]!

Singing the word "birthday," especially on a higher note, can cause havoc, so let's get this clear right away! The lower notes don't suffer as much since they are around our speaking voice, which is easier to sing, but the same rule applies to them, so here we go!

HOW TO SING AN AMERICAN "R"

Singing the [r] of "Birthday"

Singing an American [r], even when English is your native language, has an important rule no matter what style you're singing in – classical, jazz, pop, rock, Broadway. You see, the American [r] has a harsh "rrrrrr" sound, and I don't mean rolling your "r" like we've been doing on the Tongue Trills, "Drrrr." If you sing on this consonant, the sound can get stuck in your throat. Words like "mother," "father," "brother," "turkey," "birthday," and... "tarrier."

Drill Ye Tarriers Drill
High School Advanced Band Becomes a Choir

At first, I shunned the musical theater department in my public high school. That must've been my "good girl" way to rebel. I didn't want to follow the *exact* path my father wanted for me – to be a professional singer like he had wished to be. So, instead, I kept up with studying the flute. (*That'll show him!* – Yeah, right.) I had started private flute lessons when I was nine and had since upgraded to an amazing teacher, Merrill Jordan. (When I auditioned for Mr. Jordan at nine years old, he insisted that I take three years of piano lessons before I could study with him. I did it.) Merrill Jordan was the First Chair Flutist with the San Francisco Symphony. More importantly for my benefit he was a gifted teacher. Mr. Jordan was my first important classical master who helped me become a real musician.

My hard work in those flute lessons paid off. My first semester as a high school freshman, to the chagrin of the upper-classmen, I auditioned and landed the position of First Chair in the Advanced Band flute section.

I was happy to be a part of that band of misfits, about forty guys and gals from both sides of the tracks – but together, we all belonged to music. Then, one band practice, the trajectory of my young musical life was changed: The head of *all* of the choirs and musical theatre productions, JD Nichols, paid us a visit. Our band leader passed his baton to Mr. Nichols as we were handed sheet music – an old American Irish folk song called *Drill Ye Tarriers Drill*. Mr. Nichols said that the entire Advanced Band had to now *sing* as a choir in four-part harmony – that singing would make us better musicians. To this day, I can still sing the hook of that song: *Drill ye tarriers drill, oh drill ye tarriers drill!* (And it's an octave leap!)

Singing as a choir was so much fun! But what blew my mind was how Mr. Nichols made us all *pronounce* the word *tarriers*. I couldn't believe my ears! He said that we were not to say [r] – *at all*! We could say the first [t] of *tarriers* – then just the vowels until the final "s" of *tarriers* that sounds like [z].

ta – r̶r̶ i – e r̶ z

In the IPA (international Phonetic Alphabet) it is spelled like this:

tarriers = [tæ – i – ə z]

The IPA symbol for the "er" in *tarriers* is an upside-down "e." **[ə]** is called a **"shwa."** The shwa is a neutral vowel that's unstressed in English like the ending vowel in *sofa* and the "ir" and "u" vowels in *circus*. I like to think of an overexaggerated British accent saying "mother" and "father" – Don't pronounce the [r] at all. Only a shwa [ə]. For our work, as you exaggerate a British accent, also exaggerate opening your mouth with your lips in a kind of vertical pucker as you say [ə] instead of "er." Give it a try:

mother = moth[ə]
father = fath[ə]
brother = broth[ə]
turkey = t[ə]key

Now say tarriers:
ta – [i]– [ə] z

If it's easier for you, think of pronouncing tarriers like this:
ta – ꞃꞃ i – e ꞃ z

Why am i telling you all this?

I'm telling you this fun story (I hope it's fun!) to let you know about how to sing the word *birthday* in our version of "Happy Birthday." NO [r]! (There are times in other songs and styles where a smidge of [r] is appropriate – but not here. We'll cover that in Part II.)

IPA spelling for *birthday:*
[b ə θ deɪ]

To make it easy, let's think of pronouncing the phrase like this:

Happy b [ə] thday!
No [r], and pucker your lips on [ə]

Say it with me:
Happy bəthday!

This pronunciation of **bəthday** will always be executed on the high note octave leap. For the lower notes of *Happy birthday to you* that live around your mouth and speaking voice, just be sure not to hit the [r] hard. NOT *Happy birrrthday.* The lower notes being closer to our speaking voice don't have the same vocal issues in pronouncing the [r] as the higher notes. In any case, the shwa [ə] for "er" is a new rule you can take with you on all of your songs.

There are of course exceptions to every rule. But this rule to NOT sing the [r] is one that will help you in all of your songs.

When you sing these words without the [r], it sounds like there is a perfect [r] in the word. It's magic!

LET'S GET BACK TO HAPPY BIRTHDAY!

The first two notes of the **next phrase** of the song begin with an OCTAVE LEAP!

As you jump the octave leap, go from the **Floor** at your mouth on *Happy* and up immediately to the **Floor** around your eyes on **_bəthday_**.

Don't forget to use the shwa vowel [ə] when you sing the octave leap on birthday – no [r].

GIVE IT A TRY!

Happy birthday dear **(your person's name)**

- See you **Personalization** on your **Fourth Wall**
- Take an easy inhale – **The Breath**

- As you leap up the octave on Happy **bəth**-day, start Happy around the **Floor** at your mouth and send birthday up to the **Floor** around your eyes
- Then come down the **Floors** as you finish the phrase

WHAT ARE YOU AWARE OF?

Did you "see" your person on your **Fourth Wall**? Did you sing *birthday* with the shwa vowel [ə] instead of [r]? Bravo!

THE LAST PHRASE

The **last phrase** of the song you'll sing somewhere around your cheeks:

LET'S DO THIS!

Get ready to sing "Happy Birthday" using all the elements we've done so far: **The Breath**, **Support**, **Resonance**, **Personalization**, **Fourth Wall**, and **Floors**.

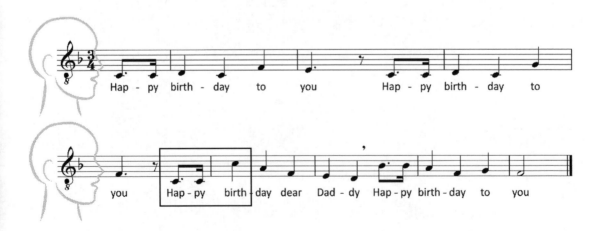

GIVE IT A TRY!

- Think of the person who you'd love to see today — They are far away, you miss them so much, and it's their birthday

- Put your **Personalization** on the central point of your **Fourth Wall**

- Take an easy inhale, **The Breath** —the tummy releases OUT

- Initiate the exhale **Support** from your bellybutton — swinging IN

- Send the song "Happy Birthday" to your person

- Say the shwa vowel [ə] for bəthday

- As you sing the melody of "Happy Birthday," be aware of the **Floors** as you go up and down the octave scale — from your mouth up to around your eyes

WHAT ARE YOU AWARE OF?

Did you "see" your **Personalization** on the **Fourth Wall**? Did you send "Happy Birthday" to your person? Did you pucker your lips on *bəth*? Did you feel the *sensation of vibration* **Resonance** on the **Floors** from your mouth up to around your eyes as you sang "Happy Birthday?" Did any emotions come up? Don't clean up! Bravo!

You just connected all the elements we've done so far: **The Breath, Support, Resonance, Personalization, Fourth Wall,** and **Floors**. Excellent work!

CONFUSING PHRASES – FLOORS

Let's revisit the *Confusing Phrases* from the beginning of the chapter and get them clear.

"What have you been taught or heard about increasing your range?"

CONFUSING PHRASES – FLOORS:

1. "Listen to the pitches as you go up the scale"

2. "Sing as if you are yawning"

3. "Push your voice down for low notes"

4. "Strengthen your vocal cords"

Let's examine each one:

1. "Listen to the pitches as you go up the scale." I have first-hand experience from trying to do this. I mean, nobody told me to do it – but it seemed to me like a good way to make my voice perfect for an opera audition. Not so much.

   When I was at Stanford University, I was auditioning for my first opera, Puccini's *Gianni Schicchi*, to play the role of Loretta who sings the famous aria, *O mio babbino caro*. (Octave leaps everywhere!) Even though I was studying privately and was a member of the elite university choir, Chorale (only two sopranos), at twenty-years-old I felt like a beginner when it came to opera. I certainly wasn't a master of my technique. (I hadn't been taught about the Floors yet.) I worried about my high notes, especially when I was nervous. A famous conductor and violinist, Andor Toth, was our brand-new professor in the music department at Stanford. He oversaw the new opera program, so my audition was solely for him. Professor Toth had never heard me sing, so I really wanted to impress him. I decided to focus on my pitches up and down the scale of *O mio babbino caro* to make sure my voice was perfect. After my audition, Professor Toth gave me my feedback: The maestro said that I was *pitchy*. The term *pitchy* means that my singing wasn't in tune – it waivered both sharp and flat throughout the entire aria. Andor Toth's critique stayed with me. I felt pretty low about it. I decided to "fix" the problem and to keep *listening* to my voice to make sure I was in tune and NOT *pitchy*. The next day I had a Chorale rehearsal. My wonderful conductor of the group, Dr. William Ramsey, came up to me after rehearsal. This is what he said:

"Mary, I understand that at your audition yesterday Andor Toth told you that you were out of pitch. Mary, in all the years I've worked with you, I've never heard you out of pitch. But, today at rehearsal, for the first time, you were in fact – pitchy. Mary, you have great pitch! You don't have any problems with pitch! Please...forget about it!"

I did forget about it. And I didn't have any problems with pitch again. I was cast as the understudy to Loretta in the opera. I went on once during the three-week run. After my performance, I was given my feedback: Andor Toth wished that he had given me the part.

The moral of the story: Don't listen to your voice while singing. It will give you pitch problems.

2. "Sing as if you are yawning." This command baffles me. When we sing, we want the throat to be in its natural state. Trying to create a bigger space in your throat by yawning just adds tension to your instrument before you even begin. Please, don't do it.

3. "Push your voice down for low notes." There may be a time for a funny character sound when you'd like to "push your voice down for the low notes." Otherwise, to have the easiest low notes that resonate beautifully, think of your lowest notes living on the lowest Floor – around your mouth. You'll be shocked how much easier it is to sing your lowest notes.

4. "Strengthen your vocal cords." It's true that the vocal cords are muscles. We often think of strengthening our muscles at the gym – your arms, your legs, your abs. But the heart is also a muscle, and although it benefits from exersice, you wouldn't deliberately focus on strengthening it. The heart is an involuntary muscle and beats freely without you thinking about it. The vocal cords also move without your direct thought. In physics, quantum theory says that when you observe a molecule, it changes the state of that molecule. We don't want to observe and thus change the natural state of our vocal cords. We want the cords to be free to do their job naturally without any extraneous effort. If you try to "strengthen" your vocal cords by thinking about making them stronger in your throat, you'll feel tension in your throat and your singing will suffer. (Even thinking about trying to strengthen my vocal cords in my throat right now as I write this, I suddenly have a lump in my throat!) Instead, to have more vocal stamina and more vocal range, your focus should be on connecting **The Breath** and **Support** to the **Resonance** on the **Floors** of your instrument. You'll feel vocal freedom and you'll be able to sing for hours on end without fatigue!

Organize yourself... Please check off **Floors**.

THE REVOLUTIONARY SEND

VOICE TECHNIQUE SIDE	EMOTIONAL LIFE SIDE
1. The Breath	1. Personalization
2. Support	2. Fourth Wall
3. Resonance	**3. Sensory Condition**
4. Floors	**4. Need**
5. Pyramid	**5. Action**

It's time for the final element on our Voice Technique Side, **Pyramid**. Layering the image of the **Floors** on top of the Front Passage **Resonance** was the first step to discovering your range. Now layering the image of the **Pyramid** on top of the **Floors** of the Front Passage will be the ultimate step for your high notes to soar!

chapter seven

PYRAMID

NICOLE KIDMAN

Do you think I can <u>really</u> sing?

I was walking down Central Park West on a blustery November afternoon looking for Sting's apartment. The numbers on the buildings were descending by two. Finally, two large glass doors with a number that matched the scribbles on the crumpled paper in my sweaty hand came into view. As I pushed the metal knob of the door, a gust of wind slammed the glass and I stumbled into the lobby. A handsome but very serious looking doorman sat behind a boat-sized wooden desk like the captain of his yacht. He threw a snide glance my way as I giggled at my wind-blown self.

"May I help you?" he curtly asked.

"Felicia, please," I tossed off as casually as I could.

"Just a minute."

We were both sharing a secret code in the name "Felicia," and we looked as cool as two Secret Service agents protecting the President. The doorman phoned upstairs and pointed down the hall. "Second floor." I smiled, trying not to look nervous as I walked the long marble hallway in my new autumn boots. The elevator doors opened. I entered and pushed the button – second floor.

I took the short ride up, and the elevator doors opened again. Right there, without a foyer or anything, was a breathtaking sight: gorgeous wooden beams, contemporary art, and spacious areas with lots of inviting couches and comfy pillows. Felicia greeted me.

"Hi there," she said. "Come this way. I guess I'll take you to the piano. That's where you're going to work, right?"

"Yes, the piano is the perfect place."

Felicia guided me to the grand piano in the even grander living room and left me alone in the stillness. The room was silent, but I was happy to sit on Sting's piano bench, imagining him creating *Fields of Gold* or maybe *Every Little Thing* on this very keyboard.

Then, as if a warm breeze entered, the energy of the room changed. A tall, blonde figure appeared from around the corner. Dressed in sleek, black running pants and a white tank top, she looked happy to meet me.

"Hi. I'm Nicole. Sorry I'm late – I just got back from my run. I'm nervous because this is my first voice lesson ever."

Nicole Kidman was starring in her Broadway debut, *The Blue Room* and garnering rave reviews. She and her family were now part-time New Yorkers, calling Sting's place home for the time being.

"So, you have an audition coming up," I said. It was easy to talk to her. Her eyes were so warm and honest.

"Yes! For Baz Luhrmann. We're friends. He has a new movie called *Moulin Rouge* and he thinks I'm right for it, but he wants to know if I can *really* sing. You think I can *really* sing?"

I knew what Nicole meant. She was worried about the *sound* of her voice. Just hearing Nicole speak, I knew she had the gift of a *beautiful* sound. And, Nicole already had something special – her craft as an actress was superb. Connecting Nicole's true singing voice *with* her exquisite acting would be the key for her confidence to "*really* sing" for Baz Luhrmann.

It was now my job to give Nicole voice technique, so her voice was free in her entire range. We began with the first three elements on the Voice Technique Side of my method: The Breath, Support, and Resonance. Fortunately, these three elements were easy for Nicole:

1. <u>The Breath:</u> To have complete access to her emotions for acting, breathing as the body works was essential – Nicole had it.

2. <u>Support:</u> Bringing the bellybutton IN for her Support was also natural, though now, learning the exact science of Support for her entire range as a "singer," Nicole could depend on it.

3. <u>Resonance:</u> Nicole's Australian accent was a gift – her Resonance was already vibrating forward in her Front Passage resonators – no vocal fry to worry about.

With those first three elements in place, Nicole was ready to head up the scale. I gave her my technical instructions:

"Sing up the Floors of the Front Passage using the shape of a Pyramid as your guide. Think of the size of the vibration of each note getting *smaller and smaller* as you sing *higher and higher*." I led Nicole up the scale. Her voice was soaring. She not only conquered the enviable high C, but she kept going! "Nicole! You just hit a high E!"

"Is that good?"

"That's not only good, it's exceptional! What a range you have. You'd better start bragging about it!"

We worked for two months on Nicole's audition material. The day finally arrived! She had her audition for Baz Luhrmann. Nicole called me later to tell me how it went. Wouldn't you know, the first thing Baz said when she walked in the door was, "I hear you can hit a high E!" High notes certainly aren't the *only* important part of singing, but sometimes they can help clinch the job.

Nicole's question hovered in my head. "You think I can *really* sing?"

"Yup Nicole, I think you can *really* sing."

Nicole Kidman was cast in the role of Satine. She was nominated for an Oscar and won a Golden Globe award for her performance in *Moulin Rouge*.

PYRAMID

5. Voice Technique Side

PYRAMID – The Physics of High Notes

The Goal: To apply the physics of high notes so that you can hit the highest notes in your range effortlessly.

Why This Is Important: Let's face it, high notes are impressive.

What Has To Change: To sing high notes, you must understand the physics of high notes. You already know about **Resonance** and **Floors**. Now you'll add yet another layer on top of the **Floors –** the image of a **Pyramid**. As you sing *higher and higher* up the **Floors** of the Front Passage, you will be aware that the *size* of the vibration of each note gets *smaller and smaller* through the shape of a **Pyramid**. Because this method is bound by physics, your high notes will become effortless.

"What have you been taught or heard about how to sing high notes?"

That's the next question I ask my new students during their first voice lesson. Here are some of their responses.

CONFUSING PHRASES – PYRAMID:

1. "Lift your soft palate"
2. "Keep your larynx low"
3. "Open your throat wider"
4. "Lift your forehead"
5. "Use *Placement* – as in *to place* your voice"

We will revisit these *Confusing Phrases* at the end of the chapter. First, let's learn about the Pyramid and how to sing high notes effortlessly.

This is a very intense chapter with tons of information – so, buckle up!

THE PHYSICS OF HIGH NOTES

Let's take a scientific look at your vocal instrument:

1. <u>The Vocal Cords:</u> When your voice is at rest or when you're speaking, the vocal cords are in their natural size and state. As you sing down the scale, the vocal cords become shorter, thicker, and vibrate more slowly. Then, as you sing up the scale, the vocal cords elongate, stretching thinner, and they vibrate more quickly.

2. <u>Size Matters:</u> Physics tells us that as the size of a cavity gets smaller, the pitch gets higher. We want to use that science to help us nail high notes.

To understand the size of the cavity and pitch better, let's do "the bottle check." Here are two cola bottles. The bottle on the left has more cola in it and *less* space. The bottle on the right has less cola and *more space.* If you blow into each bottle (like blowing into a flute), which one will have the *higher* pitch?

If you said that the bottle on the left will have the higher pitch, you're correct! **The smaller the space in the bottle, the higher the note.**

So, the question is, as a singer, what do you do with this information? How do you apply the *physics* of high notes to *sing* high notes?

1. **More Support:** Because the vocal cords elongate, stretch thinner, and vibrate faster for the high notes, as the singer, you need even more **Support** activated to sustain the quicker vibration.

   Here's how: You already know how to swing the bellybutton IN with the energy of two balls spinning around each other for your **Support** – Now, you'll add more **Support** by thinking of the two balls *zipping* around each other *faster and faster* as you go UP the scale *higher and higher.*

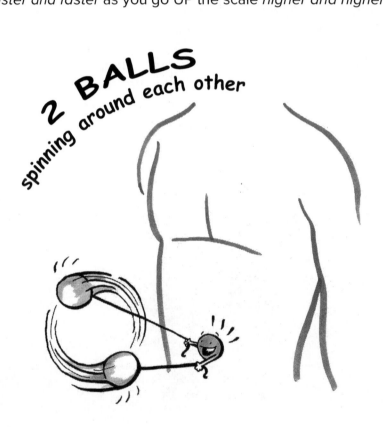

2. **Size Matters:** We know from science (remember "the bottle check") that the pitch naturally gets higher as the air cavity gets smaller. As singers, we don't want to put our attention on the structure of the cavity. (*Quantum theory tells us if we observe a molecule, it changes the state of the molecule.*) Instead, as you sing UP the scale, be aware of the vibration of each note spinning faster and faster as you sing higher and higher. At the same time, because the cavity becomes smaller for higher notes, the size of the vibration will feel smaller as you sing up the scale. To accommodate this easily, think of singing up the **Floors** of the Front Passage **Resonance** in the shape of a **Pyramid**.

Welcome to the PYRAMID

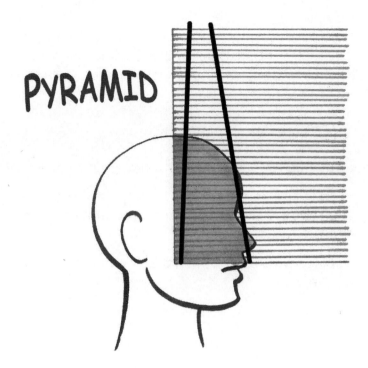

*As you can see in the picture above, the image of the **Floors** is layered on top of the Front Passage **Resonance**, and the image of the **Pyramid** is layered on top of the **Floors**.*

Singing up the Floors through the shape of a Pyramid is like a guitarist guiding their fingers up the frets of their guitar. For the guitarist, the smaller space for the higher notes is already activated just by the position of their fingers: *The shorter the length of the string, the higher the rate of vibration, and the higher the note.* **It's fun to point out that as singers, we have a higher quality instrument than a guitar: Our cavity gets smaller as we sing higher notes – but the guitar's cavity remains the same. Maybe that's why on the acoustic guitar the highest notes can sound tinny: The hollow body of the guitar helps** *low* **notes resonate, but because the cavity doesn't become smaller for the higher notes, there aren't as many overtones activated for those high pitches. As singers, we don't use our fingers to sing. Instead, we mentally guide the voice up the Floors of the Front Passage through the shape of the Pyramid. With this** *thought***, the cavity in our Front Passage will adjust on its own. Simply expect/imagine/be aware that the space for the higher notes becomes smaller. That's enough. Because we are integrating the physics of high notes, the high notes become effortless.**

THE LIP TRILL EXERCISE

In the past chapters, you have done both the Tongue Trill and Lip Trill Exercises. We are now going to concentrate only on the Lip Trill Exercise. (If you prefer the Tongue Trill Exercise, you can always apply the Tongue Trill to the Lip Trill Exercises any time you like.)

Why I love the lip trill exercise:

- It's a quick warm-up for both your voice *and* your body – you are a singing athlete

- Even if you don't do the exercise correctly, you won't hurt your voice – you're singing with training wheels

- If you're in a place where others might be bothered by sound, this exercise can be done discretely

- Whatever high note you can Lip Trill, you will be able to *sing* with practice

The beauty of the Lip Trill Exercise is that you can vocalize with all five elements of my voice technique, but without opening your mouth. In other words, it's easier. Whatever high note you reach through the Lip Trill Exercise, is your actual range. It may take practice to sing it in full voice, but you got it!

Simone

As the vocal coach to some of the leading players in Elton John's Broadway musical, *Aida*, I worked with Simone (Nina Simone's daughter) who took over the title role. Simone loved the Lip Trill Exercise. Because she was singing up to eight shows a week, her voice was *not* in need of a big warm-up before each show. As the old adage goes, *"don't leave your voice in the practice room."* One day, Simone turned to me before our work session and said, "Mary, I do a couple of Lip Trills and then walk out on stage!" I was thrilled! Simone understood that she could get a big payoff with this simple exercise.

I do the Lip Trill Exercise in the shower, waiting for the subway, in the car, or even walking down the street. I can warm-up my voice anywhere with the Lip Trill. Give it a whirl! You might like it too.

QUICK LIP TRILL

AS HIGH AS YOU CAN GO!

You already know how to slide the Lip Trill straight UP and DOWN the **Floors** of the Front Passage. Now, add the thought of guiding the Lip Trill as high as you can go up the **Floors** in the shape of a **Pyramid** and back down again. Think of the space getting *smaller and smaller* as you slide the Lip Trill *higher and higher* up above your head. Be sure to add the knee bend and surrender your head and upper torso as you go UP the scale. Then, as you come back down the scale, slide the Lip Trill down the **Floors** through the **Pyramid**, and return to standing.

PUT IT ON YOUR FEET!

- Stand and see your **Personalization** on your **Fourth Wall**

- Take an easy **Silent Breath** inhale

- As you swing the bellybutton IN for your **Support**, start on a *low note* vibrating around your mouth as you send the Lip Trill to your person

- Slide the Lip Trill straight UP the **Floors** of your Front Passage in the shape of a **Pyramid** – the space gets *smaller and smaller* as you trill *higher and higher*

- The higher you go, increase the **Support** by swinging the bellybutton IN with the energy of two balls spinning around each other *faster and faster*

- As you guide the Lip Trill up the **Pyramid** as high as you can go, 1) take a big knee bend as the bellybutton swings IN, and 2) at the same time, surrender your head and "*dive to the floor*" (figuratively) – or think of flopping over like a rag doll completely releasing the neck and upper torso

- Then slide the Lip Trill back down the scale, guiding the vibration through the **Pyramid** – return to standing and bring your head back up to see your **Personalization** on the **Fourth Wall**

PYRAMID

> **WHAT ARE YOU AWARE OF?**
>
> How did it go? Did you bend your knees and *dive to the floor*? Did you flop over like a rag doll? That's a new way of releasing the upper torso. You just jumped in! If you got it, great! If you still have more questions, let's keep going. Either way, stay with me here. Every time I explain the exercises (even now), I get to review the information myself — which keeps *my* instrument fresh too. Let's do this!

We Go Through It, Not Around It

Julia Roberts

I once heard Oscar Award–winning actress Julia Roberts say that her favorite quote is *"we go through it, not around it."* I love this advice for living life. *Experiencing* the journey on the way to your goal brings the valuable lessons. This sage advice is also helpful for the Lip Trill Exercise.

So often I hear students *skip around* the middle notes in the Lip Trill Exercise and only aim for the *high* note. The ego mind is saying, "If I can reach the high note, I've done my job. The goal is accomplished." Actually, that's not the point.

It's great to have your eye on the prize, but your definition of *the prize* must change. High notes may be an important part of your instrument, but *every* note well lived is the prize that makes the high note special. (Repeat this paragraph to yourself. It's important.)

As you slide your trilling lips up and down the scale, remember, you must go *through* the vibration of *every* note on *every* Floor of the Front Passage. Don't skip any notes, and don't skip any Floors. Enjoy the journey up and down the Pyramid.

Feel free to try the QUICK LIP TRILL again! Make sure you *go through it, not around it.*

> **Success is a journey, not a destination – Arthur Ashe**

VOCAL CATEGORIES
Your Range

To find out what the highest notes are in *your* range, we'll be singing next a Two-Octave Lip Trill Exercise. But first, let's cover a popular topic: your vocal category.

I have found that many people are obsessed about their exact vocal category. It may be helpful knowing the basic category, but please, don't get overwhelmed with the label of your voice. If you *decide* what your vocal range is before exploring the possibilities, you may be cutting yourself short of your true potential. Remember, you are one-of-a-kind!

Here are the general categories. Except where noted, they are meant for every genre and style of singing:

If you have a naturally high voice:

- The vocal category for women and children is **soprano**

- The vocal category for men is **tenor**

- If you have a naturally high voice, you'll probably be singing two octaves up to high C (and beyond) with the Lip Trill Exercise

If your voice is lower:

- The vocal category for women and children is **alto**; for women is **mezzo soprano**; or in certain styles for women is **belter**

- The vocal category for men is **baritone**

- If you have a lower voice, high G, high A, or high B♭ could be the highest notes in your range with the Lip Trill Exercise

The lowest voices are more rare:

- The vocal category for women is **contralto**

- The vocal category for men is **bass**

- For these lower voices, high G could be the top of your range with the Lip Trill Exercise

If you don't know your range, don't worry! Just give it a try! And if you do know your vocal category, get ready. You might surprise yourself with even higher notes than I listed. That's what the **Pyramid** can do!

THE ATTIC & TINKER BELL
Hitting the High Notes

When singing your highest notes, the **Floors** way up in the **Pyramid** will be so high that I call it the **ATTIC**. The bellybutton swinging IN will have such a *quick zippy energy* that I call it the Disney character **Tinker Bell**.

Now let's prepare your *highest notes* for a two-octave Lip Trill Exercise. As you trill your lips, *imagine* an itty-bitty space in the **Attic** of your **Pyramid**. Your bellybutton swings IN like *two balls zipping around each* other with the lightning speed of **Tinker Bell**.

GIVE IT A TRY!

Just for fun, do a quick super HIGH Lip Trill now! *Zip* the bellybutton IN! Trill your highest notes in the **Attic** with **Tinker Bell** energy! **Got it? Ready!**

TWO-OCTAVE LIP TRILL EXERCISE
"Ssssss" with Five-Note Phrase

LET'S DO THIS!

Now you're ready for the **Two-Octave Lip Trill Exercise**, from middle C, going all the way up to high C, and back down again to middle C. You'll say "Ssssss" and then Lip Trill the five-note phrase going up by half steps. If high C feels too high for you, just go up to where it's comfortable and back down again. If you can go higher than high C, go for it! In this exercise, you will find out *your* range today!

GIVE IT A TRY!

- See your **Personalization** on your **Fourth Wall**

- Take an easy inhale – **The Breath**

- As you exhale with the **Support**, your bellybutton swings IN on **"Ssssss"**

- Now take a *new* **Breath** – then swing the bellybutton IN and slide the Lip Trill UP the five-note phrase

- As you slide UP the first five notes of the phrase, 1) bend your knees, and 2) at the same time, surrender your head *diving to the floor,* or flopping over like a rag doll, or nodding "yes" as you completely release the neck and upper torso – whichever feels more comfortable

- As you slide the Lip Trill back down the five-note phrase, stand straight UP and bring your head back up to see your person on the **Fourth Wall**

- As you go up half-step by half-step in the two-octave scale, guide the Lip Trill vibration up the **Floors** in the shape of a **Pyramid**

- As you climb higher and higher, *expect* the higher notes to become *smaller and smaller* living in the tight space of the **Attic** in the **Pyramid** – the image of the two balls will spin *faster and faster* with the lightning speed of **Tinker Bell** from your **Super Bellybutton Support** all the way up to high C

- Then, as you descend the **Floors** in the shape of the **Pyramid**, the belly-button continues to swing IN *leading* the tone, but the speed of the two balls spinning around each other slows down little by little as you make your way back to middle C

PYRAMID

SING

As you keep practicing the Lip Trill, be aware of adjusting the pressure of your bellybutton swinging IN throughout your entire range: As you start with the lowest notes around your mouth, think of the imaginary balls spinning around each other with a long and slow pressure – then speeding up as you climb the Floors through the Pyramid – all the way up to the Attic with the lightning speed of Tinker Bell.

HITTING THE HIGH NOTES
High Notes vs. Low Notes

Now it's time to use all the information you've learned about Lip Trilling UP and DOWN the Pyramid and apply it to hitting your high notes. But first, beware! Don't forget the low notes!

High Note Envy
Judee

When I met my student Judee, she had a lovely warm mezzo soprano voice. As a successful composer, she wrote songs for her voice, but never challenged herself with high notes. Judee decided to seriously explore her high notes to expand her range and repertoire – and she had them. I'd take her vocal exercises up and up the scale as her high notes soared. But then, coming back down the scale, I suddenly heard each lower note become thinner and weaker – not the beautiful rich timber of her mezzo soprano. What was happening?

Then it came to me: HIGH NOTE ENVY!

Judee was so committed to those high notes that she unknowingly sang *every note as if* it was high – on a high Floor in a small space in her Pyramid. She wasn't utilizing the wider Pyramid shape for her lower notes on the lower Floors. The result? Judee's high notes soared, but her lower notes sounded weak and thin. With my instruction, Judee adjusted the lower notes to the fuller space of the Pyramid returning to her rich mezzo soprano. Now she had a big range and beautiful voice from top to bottom. No more High Note Envy!

> **HIGH NOTE ENVY:** Those who are so focused on singing high notes that they unknowingly sing all the notes in their range as if they were high notes. Honor your full range. Don't envy the high notes.

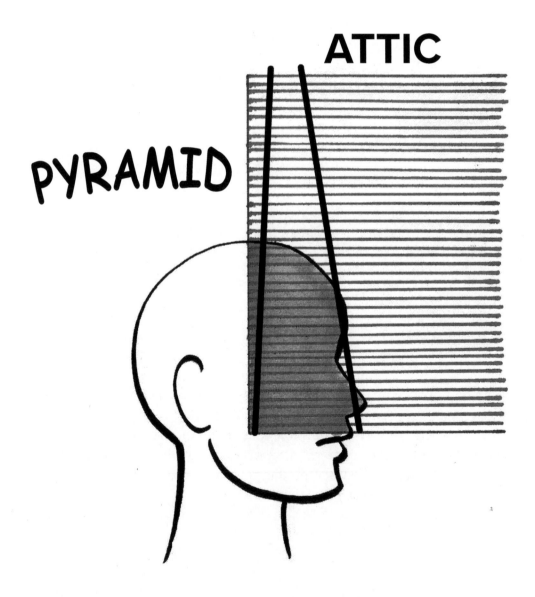

PREP THROWING THE BALL

If you have a friend with you, you can do this exercise as partners. Stand across from each other ready to "play catch" with an imaginary ball. Otherwise, "play catch" with the person you'd love to see today on your **Fourth Wall**.

You'll just be **SPEAKING** in this exercise on elongated vowels, as in:

Haaaap – yyyyy B ə ə ə ə ə th – daaaaay

Don't forget the shwa vowel [ə] in **B ə ə ə ə ə th – daaaaay**

GIVE IT A TRY!

- Stand and see your person on your **Fourth Wall**

- Pretend you have a ball in your hand ready to "play catch"

- If you're throwing the ball right-handed, turn sideways putting your left shoulder toward your person and your right shoulder back

- If you're throwing the ball left-handed, turn sideways and put your right shoulder toward your person and your left shoulder back

- Now practice throwing the ball overhand to your person, 1) With the ball just in your hand, say **Haaaap – yyyyy** 2) then take a big step forward with your front foot, 3) and *throw* the ball *overhand* in slow motion to your person saying B ə ə ə ə ə th – daaaaay as your person "catches" the ball

- If you have a partner, they will now throw the ball back to you and you catch the ball

- Repeat

WHAT ARE YOU AWARE OF?

Are you able to throw the imaginary ball *overhand* to your person as you speak with elongated vowels **Haaaap – yyyyy B ə ə ə ə ə th – daaaaay**?

To sing, we must SEND your voice on vowels. Now that you've extended those vowels throwing the ball while SPEAKING, it's time to SING through those vowels up and back down the scale. Here we go!

HAPPY BIRTHDAY UP & DOWN 5ths EXERCISE

I love preparing songs with exercises using the *text* from that song. That's just what we are going to do with "Happy Birthday." In this next exercise you will SING the words *Happy Birthday* up and down 5ths from middle C all the way up two octaves to high C while *throwing the ball*. If high C feels too high for you, just go up to where it's comfortable and back down again. If you can go higher than high C, go for it!

SING THE HIGH NOTES "ON TOP"

As you jump up to the high 5th of each phrase, *think* of entering each high note singing *Bəth* of "Birthday" ON TOP. Throwing the ball *overhand* is a huge help to remind you of this instruction. But don't forget the lower notes too on the lower Floors of your Pyramid. No High Note Envy!

GIVE IT A TRY!

- Stand and see your partner or person on your **Fourth Wall** while prepping the imaginary ball in your hand

- Keep seeing your person and take an easy inhale – **The Breath**

- Initiate the **Support** from your Super Bellybutton swinging IN

- Sing **Happy**

- Then throw the ball overhand to your person taking a big step forward with your front foot singing **B ə ə ə ə ə th** on the high 5th

- Keep throwing the ball as you finish down the 5th with **day**, as your person catches the ball

- If you have a partner, now they sing and throw the imaginary ball back to you and you catch the ball – keep going back and forth up the scale in half steps

- If you are alone, keep going up the scale throwing to your person on your **Fourth Wall** – keep singing half steps up the **Floors** of your Front Passage in the shape of the **Pyramid**

- Every time you throw the ball to the high 5th sing *Bəth* of "Birthday" ON TOP

- Be sure to come back DOWN the Pyramid for your lower notes on the lower Floors – No High Note Envy

WHAT ARE YOU AWARE OF?

Did you throw the ball *overhand* to your person and discover the lower and higher **Floors** through the shape of the **Pyramid**? Did you enter the high 5th ON TOP? Did you come back DOWN the Pyramid, so your lower notes lived on the lower Floors? No High Note Envy!

PYRAMID

HAPPY BIRTHDAY IN A HIGH KEY
Pyramid, Attic, Tinker Bell

To practice using the **Pyramid** in a song, now let's sing "Happy Birthday" in a high key applying the **Attic** and **Tinker Bell's** *zippy* energy.

This written version goes up to high G. Feel free to raise or lower the key as you like. As long as it is high in your range, you are doing the exercise correctly. This is NOT a final performance or supposed to be your chosen comfortable key. This is to *practice* the higher notes in the **Attic** with the *zippy* energy of **Tinker Bell**.

GIVE IT A TRY!

- Stand and see your **Personalization** on the **Fourth Wall**

- Before you sing, *think* of starting the song on the **Floors** around your cheeks and eyes and **SPEAK** the words there – *Happy birthday to you*

- Now take an easy **Silent Breath** inhale

- Swing your bellybutton IN and SING the first two phrases to your person on your **Fourth Wall**, *Happy birthday to you* (inhale) *Happy birthday to you*

- Next, as you make the octave leap, increase the *zippy* Tinker Bell energy of your **Super Bellybutton**, throw the ball *overhand* to your person, and sing the word *bəthday* way up in the small space of the **Attic** above your head

- Be sure to enter the octave leap in the **Attic** ON TOP

- As you finish the song, bring the words back down to around your cheeks and eyes in the shape of the **Pyramid**

Hap - py birth - day to you Hap - py birth - day to you Hap - py

birth - day dear Dad - dy Hap - py birth - day to you

WHAT ARE YOU AWARE OF?

How did it feel to sing "Happy Birthday" in a high key? Did you sing the word *bərthday* way up in the **Attic**? If the space felt tiny and high, you were right! Did you sing the octave leap ON TOP? Did you add the **Super Bellybutton Support** for the **Attic** notes as if the two balls were *zipping* around each other like the lightning speed of **Tinker Bell**? This is great practice for high passages in your repertoire. Now you know how to prepare.

CONFUSING PHRASES – PYRAMID

"What have you been taught or heard about how to sing high notes?"

Let's revisit the *Confusing Phrases* from the beginning of the chapter of how to sing high notes and get the important answers:

CONFUSING PHRASES – PYRAMID:

1. "Lift your soft palate"

2. "Keep your larynx low"

3. "Open your throat wider"

4. "Lift your forehead"

5. "Use *Placement* – as in *to place* your voice"

   1. "Lift the soft palate." Some teachers tell their students to "lift the soft palate" to sing high notes. When you sing a higher note, the physical change in the throat is the vocal cords stretch thinner, and yes, the soft palate physically lifts higher. But just as I don't want you to *think* about your vocal cords vibrating while singing, I also don't want you to *think* about *lifting* the soft palate. Focusing on the physical result of the soft palate rising while singing high notes will add tension to your voice. Remember, in quantum physics there is a theory that says *when you observe a molecule, the molecule changes its state*. Instead of *thinking* about the soft palate lifting, put your attention on going up the Floors of the Front Passage in the shape of a Pyramid. That's enough.

   2. "Keep your larynx low." The larynx is the voice box that lives in your throat and houses the vocal cords. When you sing up and down the scale, the larynx does shift up and down in your throat too. Singers who struggle to reach high notes are known to try to squeeze those high notes from the throat – in turn, the larynx can sharply rise and practically "strangle" the singer. To try and solve this issue, some teachers give the command to "keep your larynx low," thus trying to fix the symptom, but not the problem. The *problem* starts at the beginning – and then there is a domino

effect: If The Breath and Support are not properly in place, free high notes are not possible. If the singer doesn't supply a smaller space for the higher notes on the higher Floor, the larynx can rise with terrible tension. Trying to *muscle* the larynx down only adds more tension. Studying all five voice technique elements of *The Revolutionary Send* — The Breath, Support, Resonance, Floors, and Pyramid — will keep the larynx *naturally* low. Your high notes will be easy, and you won't *add* tension to your throat trying to muscle the larynx into a low position.

3. "Open your throat wider." Trying to create a bigger space in your throat to sing higher notes will make the pitch flat and the tone dissipated. Worse, it may also damage your vocal cords in trying to do so. To reach the highest notes in your range, you will now imagine those notes living on the highest Floors in you Front Passage, vibrating in a *smaller* space...*not* bigger. Just the way the physics works.

4. "Lift your forehead." We often hear this command from choir directors who are trying desperately to get their choir to not sing flat (sagging below the correct pitch). In saying to the choir, *lift your forehead!* the singers *reach up* with their foreheads to lift the pitch higher. When you think about it, this command is trying to get the choir members to lift their voices to a higher Floor — maybe that's why it often works. The only problem is that physically *lifting the forehead* adds *tension* from the forehead in order to sing on pitch, which brings on physical fatigue and muted tones. I suggest that choir directors have their singers connect The Breath with the bellybutton Support (have everybody do a few "Ssssss" exercises), then connect to the Resonance ("Hmmmmm" through the Front Passage), sing some exercises going up the Floors adding *more* energy of the Super Bellybutton Support and using the shape of the Pyramid for the higher notes. The choir would sing right on pitch, and their voices would be fresh, vibrant, and gorgeous for hours on end without fatigue.

5. "Use *Placement* — as in to *place* your voice." With the terms I use, Floors and Pyramid, there certainly is a kind of *Placement* in my method. But "to place" the voice is not my favorite term. Instead of saying *place your voice*, I use words like expect and *imagine*. I want you to LET the vibration of the tone live. If you try to hold your voice "in place," there could be extra tension that inhibits the free Resonance.

MYTH: *Real singers don't need voice lessons.*

It's true, there are professional singers who claim they've never had a voice lesson – and they sound really good! I call them Inspirational Singers. They trust their body as God made it – to breathe, support, and sing. They express their emotions without worry or judgment. But what about the days when these singers *don't* feel inspired? What do they do if they are suddenly a bundle of nerves for a big event, or they're singing outside in the freezing cold air, or there's someone important in the audience who they'd like to impress? I've heard these artists in stressful situations screech out of pitch and crack on high notes. I wonder, might they reconsider that lesson? For the rest of us, it is really helpful to have a set of tools like the concepts in this chapter to turn to in moments like this. We can be inspired every time.

Organize yourself – Please check off **Pyramid**.

THE REVOLUTIONARY SEND

VOICE TECHNIQUE SIDE	EMOTIONAL LIFE SIDE
1. ~~The Breath~~	1. ~~Personalization~~
2. ~~Support~~	2. ~~Fourth Wall~~
3. ~~Resonance~~	**3. Sensory Condition**
4. ~~Floors~~	**4. Need**
5. ~~Pyramid~~	**5. Action**

You now have in place ALL the elements on the Voice Technique Side of *The Revolutionary Send*: **The Breath**, **Support**, **Resonance**, **Floors**, and **Pyramid**. You're also incorporating the first two elements on the Emotional Life Side: **Personalization** and **Fourth Wall**. Great work!

Now we are ready to finish the last three elements on the Emotional Life Side: **Sensory Condition**, **Need**, and **Action**.

Get ready to bust your fear and tension with **Sensory Condition**. Let's do this!

chapter eight

SENSORY CONDITION

MISS UNIVERSE
Singing Seduction

Miss Universe's manager called me. "My client just auditioned for the role of Mimi in the movie musical, *Rent*. I'm confused: The pianist was *blown away*. But the casting director – well, she didn't say much. Though she did agree to another audition – this time for the Broadway version of *Rent* – and suggested that my client have a voice lesson. Can you help?"

I said, "Yes." Then, I called the casting director to find out what the problem was. I got my answer. "Good thing she'll be working with you, Mary...She can't sing!"

Oh, my goodness – "Blown away" and "She can't sing!" are worlds apart. I was so curious to hear her.

The next day, Miss Universe walked into my studio. I figured she'd be beautiful, and sure enough, she was knock-out gorgeous – just who they'd want to cast for the character of Mimi. We went through Mimi's famous first number, "Out Tonight." Low and behold, Miss Universe had an *amazing* pop voice! She had a beautiful tone and hit all the high notes. She had also done her homework: Her belting and phrasing were exactly that of Daphne Rubin Vega, the original Mimi. You see, it's usually the hard and fast rule for singers to learn the score of a musical just as the composer wrote it – on the paper – not as you hear it on the recording. But *Rent* is the exception to this rule. The musical director of *Rent* told me specifically, "The original cast recording of *Rent* is the template for all future casts."

Because of her beauty, powerful voice, and wonderful range, now I knew why the pianist was *blown away*. And yet, the renowned casting director said, "She can't sing!" And I knew why. As beautiful, slender, and sexy-looking as Miss Universe was, her body was jammed. There was tension in her neck, arms, hips, and legs. In other words, there was no sensuality in her body. Without the sexuality of Mimi, it clearly didn't matter to the casting director what her voice could do with the notes.

It dawned on me that Miss Universe had competed for years in bathing suits and glamorous gowns, showing off her figure, while being sure never to come across to the pageant judges as sexually "crude." However, in *Rent*, the character of Mimi has a devastating need for sexual attention and is on the prowl during "Out Tonight." But Miss Universe wouldn't go there. It was too scary for her to be overtly sexy. I didn't know exactly *why* she was scared, but I had to think of a way for Miss Universe to release her body, so she'd expose her sexuality while singing. Sensory Condition to the rescue! And the best sensation to use for sensuality? Oil.

"While you sing, feel the *sensation of oil* running down your body. Imagine the oil dripping from the top of your head all the way down to your toes." It worked like a charm. As Miss Universe sang, her neck, arms, hips, and legs released simply by focusing on the oil. But could she keep it up? The audition was the next day, and she had to trust this new sensation and not revert back to the muscle memory of a jammed body.

Miss Universe sang for the casting director – again. And guess what? She got the callback! Imagine that – the casting director actually changed her opinion from *She can't sing!* to sending her on to meet the creative team. That same day Miss Universe sang her final audition for the director and a room full of producers. Could Miss Universe sustain the *sensation of oil* in her work in front of all of those "judges" and keep her body free?

I received her feedback after the final audition: "She didn't *let herself go* as Mimi. She didn't get the part."

Using Sensory Condition, like the *sensation of oil*, takes practice. Just as vocal exercises, it needs to be a part of your daily routine – not just trying it once or twice. Maybe with a little more time, Miss Universe would have been able to bust through her fear and trust the new sensation. But you can be assured, Sensory Condition can be a magical tool in bringing your singing to the next level.

SENSORY CONDITION
3. Emotional Life Side

SENSORY CONDITION – Busting Fear & Tension

The Goal: To help you avoid thinking analytically and judgmentally about your voice, as in *How do I sound? Does the audience like me?* Those thoughts tighten every muscle in your body and jam both your voice and your performance. Now you'll learn how to release the body into a sensation.

Why This Is Important: When you think about the sound of your voice, or are judging your performance, not only does your body get tense and distract *you* from the story of your song, but at the same time, the *audience* becomes distracted and doesn't experience you.

What Has To Change: Instead of being overcome by fear and thoughts in your head, you'll focus on a *sensation* in your body. Sensory Condition takes you out of the analytical part of your brain that triggers fear and tension and moves you into the creative part of your brain, so you can be *in* your body and sing with vocal freedom.

FOUR EXAMPLES OF SENSORY CONDITION
Out of Your Head and Into Your Body

Let's get right to it! There are certainly hundreds of choices to use as a Sensory Condition. Here are four of my favorite examples that we will use in our exercises ahead.

1. Feel the *sensation of oil*
2. Feel the *sensation of the sun*
3. Feel the *sensation of being tipsy*
4. Step into a character

1. SENSATION OF OIL

Miss Universe

You just read about Miss Universe using the *sensation of oil* running down her body as a Sensory Condition. Now it's your turn.

GIVE IT A TRY!

STAND UP

- As you stand there, open your arms up wide and close your eyes
- Think of oil running down your body, from the top of your head, all of the way down to your toes
- BREATHE into the *sensation the oil* running down your face – neck – torso – arms – legs – feet
- Say "Hmmmmm" and chew with the *sensation* of oil on your mouth and jaw
- Feel your body reverberating with the *sensation of oil* as you say "Hmmmmm"

WHAT ARE YOU AWARE OF?

Can you feel the *sensation of oil* running down your body, and on your mouth and jaw? Your imagination is your friend. Really let yourself go and *feel* the oil. Have fun! If you want to practice the sensation, get some baby oil and rub it all over your body. You'll be ready when you want to recall this Sensory Condition.

The Magic of [m]

Have you noticed? I use the [m] consonant in our exercises – like "Hmmmmm" – and there's a good reason why. Since you say the [m] with your lips, this consonant naturally vibrates and brings your voice forward (because your lips are in the *front* of your face). Pressing your lips softly together and enjoying the vibration of [m] somewhere around your mouth and upper lip is ideal. Now, adding a Sensory Condition, like the *sensation of oil*, the [m] takes on a whole new dimension. You don't *think* about the exercise – instead, you *feel* the sensation, and your fear and tension magically disappear.

Three Tension Tweaks

The Tongue, the Jaw, the Forehead

The tongue, jaw, and forehead are the three biggest culprits of holding tension for many singers. Sensory Condition can eliminate that sneaky tension when the tongue, jaw, and forehead are jammed.

1. The Tongue
Eric Anthony Lopez

When I heard my student Eric Anthony Lopez sing for me in his first voice lesson, he was pulling his tongue way back and holding it tight in order to make the tone of his magnificent operatic voice darker, bigger, and sound older. The tongue tension actually *distorted* his voice and created a "fake" sound. When Eric released his tongue in the *sensation of oil*, his voice was twice as big and beautiful in the room, and it sounded like *his* voice – not an imposter. Eric went on to be the youngest tenor to ever sing the role of Piangi in *The Phantom of the Opera*.

2. The Jaw
Bugs Bunny

There are many reasons for jaw tension. Here are a few:

- Holding the jaw to hear your voice back in your head

- Locking the jaw (like TMJ) to emotionally "hold on" because of accumulated stress, anxiety, and anger – Think of a dog locking his jaw and growling when he's angry

- Holding the jaw as the Support for your voice

Do you see yourself in any of those examples?

Holding the jaw as the Support for the voice is what happened to my student Jeffrey Bergman. Jeffrey has been the world-renowned voice of Bugs Bunny and many animated characters in movies, commercials, and on television for decades. He came to me because for the first time in his career he had to *sing* as Bugs Bunny.

As you can imagine, the Resonance of Jeffrey's speaking voice was incredible. He could make so many different character voices applying his creative usage of the resonators in his face, throat, and head. But when Jeffrey sang for me, I saw his jaw tighten trying to *support* his voice. Turns out he didn't know about the Super Bellybutton – and with one lesson, he got it!

With Jeffrey's newfound Support and the joy of *releasing* his jaw through the *sensation of oil*, he sang as Bugs Bunny with ease. Even better, after long recording sessions of singing and reading as the animated characters, his voice didn't get tired. The Support and Sensory Condition gave Jeffrey new stamina for his voice-over work in both singing *and* speaking.

3. The Forehead
Natural Botox

Scrunching the forehead is indicative of thinking and worrying. I myself have the habit of furrowing my brow when I'm thinking. Releasing the forehead in the *sensation of oil* applies a kind of "natural Botox" so that there are no wrinkles in your forehead and more overtones can *ring* in your timbre. If you have this problem, grab some scotch tape, and put a nice large piece in the middle of your forehead while singing. Along with the *sensation of oil,* you'll be reminded not to scrunch your forehead. "Natural Botox" is the key.

LEGATO EXERCISE

Sensation of Oil

You've already done exercises with "relaxing" your tongue, and "chewing" to release your jaw. Now, as you connect the wonderful vibration of the [m] to the Legato Exercise, also imagine the *sensation of oil* on your tongue, jaw, forehead, and running down your body. You are activating the Sensory Condition with a *feeling* rather than a *thought*, and it will improve every aspect of your voice technique.

As you've done before, sing [mi me ma mo mu] as seamlessly as possible starting on middle C. Focus on the *sensation of vibration* starting with the consonant [m] and *send* that vibration to your **Personalization** on the **Fourth Wall** through each vowel smoothly and effortlessly.

GIVE IT A TRY!

[mi me ma mo mu]

RELEASE THE TONGUE, JAW, & FOREHEAD

- Stand and see your **Personalization** on the **Fourth Wall**

- Touch the tip of your tongue on the back of the bottom teeth

- Feel the *sensation of oil* on your tongue, jaw, forehead, and running down from the top of your head to the bottom of your feet

- Take an easy inhale – and then initiate the exhale with bellybutton swinging IN

- Sing [mi me ma mo mu] as you slowly *reach* to your person

- Move your jaw side to side, and release your tongue and forehead in the *sensation of oil*

- Repeat going up the scale and up the **Floors** by half steps, completely releasing your tongue, jaw, and forehead through the sensation of oil

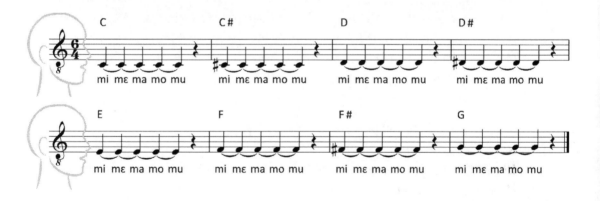

> **WHAT ARE YOU AWARE OF?**
>
> Can you *feel* the sensation of the oil? Does it feel good? Did you move the jaw side to side in the *sensation of oil*? The jaw is never *connected* to the tone. Instead, the jaw *swings away from the tone.* Feel the jaw moving and releasing in the *sensation of oil.* When you release tension, more overtones are able to *ring* in your one-of-a-kind timbre. You are now adding yet another dimension to your voice technique.

2. SENSATION OF THE SUN

Paul Newman

Susan Batson recounts a story told by her master acting teacher, Lee Strasberg, from the days she studied with him at the Actors Studio in New York City.

Young Paul Newman – that's right, the late great Oscar-winning actor – was faced with a dilemma. His body was stiff. When the stiffness took over, Paul Newman was void of his natural charisma. His acting seemed jammed up and his "X-factor" disappeared.

Lee Strasberg instructed his student to use a Sensory Condition: "Walk in the *sensation of the sun.*" Suddenly, Paul Newman's life force was literally *illuminated* by just *feeling* the sun on his face and body. The stiffness was transformed into the star quality he innately possessed, on and off camera.

Skipping Over Alice

Even though Alice had one of the most beautiful voices in my class – and the most singing experience – I kept skipping over her during our group sessions. I didn't see Alice even when she was right in front of me. It seemed a bit odd since she always had a beaming smile, positive personality, and was committed to the work.

"Alice, does this happen to you often? Do people not notice that you're there?"

"Oh yes, it happens all of the time. Maybe I'm just shy."

I told Alice the Paul Newman story and gave her the same homework to "walk in the *sensation of the sun*." We also applied the sunshine to the songs she was performing at the student showcase the following week. Alice loved it!

The week rolled around and I decided to have Alice open the show. I make sure the first singer has some prior stage experience, a beautiful voice, and confidence. Alice had done her homework perfectly. That night she wowed the crowd! Her performance was emotional and touching with a gorgeous voice and star quality that shined. After the show she ran up to me.

"Mary! I've been walking in the *sensation of the sun* all week! And let me tell you, everybody has been looking at me – and talking to me! There's even a boy that I've been too shy to talk to. Well...he came up to ME and talked to ME!" It's been the best week ever!

Not only does the Sensorial Condition help with stage presence – now you have a tool to meet new people.

GIVE IT A TRY!

STAND UP

- Imagine you are standing on your favorite sunny beach, mountain top, or any place in nature that you love

- Open your arms up wide and close your eyes

- Feel the sensation of the sun on your face – neck – torso – arms – legs – feet – the rays of the sun pouring into each molecule of your skin

- BREATHE into the sensation of the sun all over your body

- Say "Hmmmmm" through the sensation of the sun and chew

WHAT ARE YOU AWARE OF?

Do you feel the *sensation of the sun* on your body? The next time you're outside on a sunny day, try walking in the *sensation of the sun* – just like Paul Newman and Alice. That's how you practice.

Luisa in a Car

My student Luisa was driving her car in Milan when she decided to practice feeling the *sensation of the sun*. She opened her chest in the sunshine and felt the sun's rays on her face and torso. Just then, a car of rowdy boys drove by hanging out the windows blowing her kisses yelling, "Bellissima!!!"

Luisa was shocked and delighted to get immediate feedback that Sensory Condition works!

LEGATO EXERCISE
Feel the Sensation of the Sun

GIVE IT A TRY!

[mi me ma mo mu]

Now let's go back DOWN the scale with the same Legato Exercise starting on G and moving down half step by half step to C. When you sing **[mi me ma mo mu]** and feel the *sensation of the sun* on your body, you can slightly move your head and body, swaying in the sunshine as you *reach* to your person.

- See your person on the **Fourth Wall** and breathe into the *sensation of the sun* shining on your face and body

- As you sing **[mi me ma mo mu]**, reach your arm slowly to the person on your **Fourth Wall** feeling the *sensation of the sun*

- As you are reaching, sway a bit back and forth in the *sensation of the sun*

- As you sing down the scale, think of **[mi me ma mo mu]** slowing coming down the **Floors** from G around your cheeks to middle C around your mouth

WHAT ARE YOU AWARE OF?

Can you feel the *sensation of the sun* on your face and body as you slowly reaching to your **Personalization** on the **Fourth Wall**? This helps you get out of your head, into your body, and *send* your voice to your person. Remember, doing the sensory work takes practice. For more practice, keep walking in the *sensation of the sun*. And if you try it while driving like Luisa, be sure to keep your eyes on the road!

3. SENSATION OF BEING TIPSY

Marta

Marta sent me a message that she was preparing *My Funny Valentine* for her final vocal exam at an Italian conservatory. She was nervous because her teachers were telling her to sing louder. "Push your voice out!" they'd say. But all she felt was strain on her vocal cords when she tried to comply. We scheduled a private lesson.

Marta walked into the practice room in Milan looking just as I had remembered her in my class one year before. She reminded me of Audrey Hepburn in *Breakfast at Tiffany's* – both beautiful and vulnerable. (To be a singer who is *sensitive* is a gift, and Marta had it.) She sang for me. The Breath and Support were in place, and she was singing with beautiful Resonance through the Floors and Pyramid. I was happy to see that Marta had kept all five voice technique elements from our work together the previous year.

Then, the problem showed its face: Marta was checking to see if her voice was enough. Her eyes were wandering up as if she was trying to look inside her head to hear her tone. Her light and feathery body was taut and constricted, "holding on" for dear life. And, yes, just like her teachers at the conservatory said, her voice was too soft. But even with all of that tension, Marta was vulnerable. She sang from her heart.

> "Marta, you're doing so many things well. Your voice technique is great, and you're emotionally connected to the song. All we have to do now is add three acting elements to your performance that will give you a *focus* and eliminate the unwanted tension in your body so your final exam can *sing*."

I instructed Marta to put the Personalization of *her* Funny Valentine on the Fourth Wall. Now her eyes were focused on *him*, not on the sound of her own voice. I went further. "The person is far away from you, so you must *send* the song to reach him." A-ha! Now her voice was automatically louder without extraneous pushing. Then we had to conquer the real culprit – her tense body. I could feel Marta's fear of not living up to her teachers' expectations for the final exam. Sensory Condition would do the trick.

> "Marta, you're 21. Have you ever felt tipsy on alcohol? If not, you can use another high, like laughing too much, or a good conversation."
>
> "I've been tipsy on alcohol before."
>
> "And do you remember that sensation?"
>
> "Sure!"
>
> "Okay! Let's use the Sensory Condition of being tipsy on alcohol. I'll tell you what, just spin around and get dizzy. You'll feel tipsy right away." Sure enough, Marta spun around, and voilà! She was tipsy. "Alright, TIPSY Marta! See the person on your Fourth Wall and *send* the song to him. Remember, he's far away, so make sure he hears you!"

On the first try, Marta was in her full power. She saw the person to whom she was singing on her Fourth Wall, and with the sensation of alcohol making her tipsy, her body released completely. Marta was the vessel of her own, authentic version of *My Funny Valentine* – all within an hour.

Later that week, Marta passed her final exams with flying colors.

* * *

We just observed Marta in the *sensation of being tipsy.* Now it's your turn! You *don't* need to drink alcohol or to have ever had a drink! The tipsy sensation can be the high of "laughing too hard with a friend," or a "good conversation." In any event, I have found that the quickest and most fun way of feeling tipsy is to "spin around and get dizzy." Let's do this!

HAPPY BIRTHDAY BEING TIPSY

GIVE IT A TRY!

- Stand up and SPIN AROUND – (be sure to be in a safe place so if you fall you don't hit the corner of a table...no blood, please)

- Now you're dizzy and ready to go

- See your **Personalization** on the **Fourth Wall**

- Sing "Happy Birthday" to your person with the *sensation of being tipsy*

- Have fun – let the tipsy feeling take over, releasing your face – mouth – body – like you're drunk on alcohol, laughing too hard, or having a good conversation

WHAT ARE YOU AWARE OF?

Can you feel the *sensation of being tipsy*? Did that "high" feeling free you up while you were singing? You don't need to practice with alcohol. Instead, just spin around and get dizzy. That's enough.

4. STEP INTO A CHARACTER

Maria as Marilyn Monroe

Maria was an interesting case. As she sang her rendition of "Over the Rainbow" from *The Wizard of Oz* in front of the class, she held her jaw and barely moved her mouth. That's a sign of control. Maria's voice was muffled, but there was more: I found that Maria's tight jaw transformed her face. Strangely, she had a cute pout reminiscent of the 1930's child star, Shirley Temple. My diagnosis: Maria was trying to stay a little girl and not expose her femininity and sensuality as a woman.

I had an inkling that if Maria moved her mouth like a "sexy character," all of the issues would be solved in one fell swoop. You see, taking on a "character" would have Maria stepping *outside* of herself. She just might have the courage to be a grown woman as *somebody else*.

"Maria, move your mouth like you are Marilyn Monroe. It will feel too big, I know, but just give it a try."

Maria followed my instruction and dropped into the character of Marilyn Monroe, moving her mouth like the sexy "femme fatale." In that moment, Maria's lips went from tight rubber bands to a voluptuous, released mouth. Suddenly, we heard a *beautiful* tone in the room. Maria started to cry.

"I feel so *stupid* opening my mouth!"

"You don't look stupid – you look and sound wonderful!"

"I can't do it!"

Instead of trying to convince Maria myself that she just solved all of her vocal issues, I went to her twelve classmates to give her feedback. "What are you aware of when Maria sings with her mouth *moving* like Marilyn Monroe?"

The response of every student was, "Maria is a beautiful, feminine woman with a gorgeous voice."

Maria's tight jaw was a way for her to be in control, stay a child, and not expose her femininity as a woman. When it released, so did a flood of tears.

Don't Clean Up

As human beings, we hold fear and pain from past events and trauma in our bodies. Singing through those fears can be cathartic, and at the same time, reveal a more beautiful voice and a tone that is only yours. By using Sensory Condition, you have an immediate way to release those fears and reveal your true voice. If tears come up, don't clean up. Keep crying. Your freedom is on the other side.

Step Into A Character – Happy Birthday

Marilyn Monroe & Elvis Presley

Now it's your turn to "step into a character." We are heading to Chapter Ten when you'll connect "Happy Birthday" to Marilyn Monroe's performance, *Happy Birthday Mr. President*. Enjoy stepping into the "femme fatale" character of **Marilyn Monroe**. In addition, let's try it two ways! Second time around, step into a character who is more of a "stud" rather than a "femme fatale." Let's use the character of **Elvis Presley**. He too moved his mouth and body with beautiful ease and sensuality. Sing "Happy Birthday" twice having fun with each character.

GIVE IT A TRY!

- Stand as see your **Personalization** on the **Fourth Wall**

- As you stand there, feel the sensation of your mouth and body like you are the character of **Marilyn Monroe** – and then **Elvis Presley**

- Sing "Happy Birthday" to your person as if you were that character

- Have fun – let the character take over, release your face – mouth – body – like you're **Marilyn Monroe** – and then **Elvis Presley**

- Sing "Happy Birthday" all of the way to the end of the song, and stay in the character

Hap - py birth - day to you Hap - py birth - day to you Hap - py

birth - day dear Dad - dy Hap - py birth - day to you

WHAT ARE YOU AWARE OF?

Did you step into the characters of **Marilyn Monroe** and **Elvis Presley**? Could you hand over your mouth and body to the characters? Did you feel freedom in the release of giving over to the characters and not being "you?" Your imagination is your friend. And if you want to practice, walk around during the day in a character of your choice. It's an amazing actors' tool that will free your voice and bust the tension and fear that hold you back.

As we move forward, Sensory Condition will always be present when you are singing. You might love one particular sensation the best – like the *sensation of the sun*, or the *sensation of oil* – so feel free to use it for everything. That's fine. Sensory Condition is such a marvelous tool to release your body on any given day. Whether you wake up full of joy, or full of anxiety – Sensory Condition has literally got your back.

Organize yourself... Please check off **Sensory Condition**.

THE REVOLUTIONARY SEND

VOICE TECHNIQUE SIDE

1. ~~The Breath~~
2. ~~Support~~
3. ~~Resonance~~
4. ~~Floors~~
5. ~~Pyramid~~

EMOTIONAL LIFE SIDE

1. ~~Personalization~~
2. ~~Fourth Wall~~
3. ~~Sensory Condition~~
4. **Need**
5. **Action**

Now let's finish *The Revolutionary Send* components with **Need** and **Action**!

chapter nine

NEED

MARY SETRAKIAN
This One Is Personal

As my taxi from the airport crossed a spectacular bridge, I could see the luminous island of Manhattan. Yup, I sang that Frank Sinatra cliché right there in the taxi.

"If I can make it there I'll make it anywhere...It's up to you...New York... New Yoooork!"

I borrowed a temporarily vacant apartment in Greenwich Village and had a month to put a life together: find a home, a job, friends, and with any luck, my feet on a stage.

I pounded the pavement, sustaining myself with the box of rice I'd found atop the fridge. It was a great money saver and also on my diet. Discovering cooked worms in my dish was not so delightful, but I considered it extra protein and carried on.

My first week there, to my joy I auditioned and landed in the chorus of an off-Broadway repertoire company, the Light Opera of Manhattan (LOOM for short). I made $35 a week. Woo hoo! I was a working actress! Apartment hunting, I hit gold the third week. My wonderful college friend Marty had another college friend Marty who needed a roommate. Perfect! The fourth week I landed a secretary job in the mornings. The rent-free month paid off in spades.

But I still wanted Broadway.

Big River

I was waiting in line, hoping to be seen for my first Broadway audition – *Big River*– a new musical with an exciting score by Roger Miller. On Broadway, you are required to sing in all styles – legit, belt, pop, rock – and now, (drum roll) ...country. On Broadway, you also have to be in the actors' union called Equity. If you're not, you wait at the end of the audition line behind the Equity actors and hope to be seen if there's time left. That was me.

The casting director, Stanley Soble, peaked his head out of the studio and said the magic words, "I'll hear everybody today, even non-Equity." *(Yippee!)* Instead of the usual quick 16 bars, he would only hear 8 bars. Let me tell you, that's quick.

I couldn't decide what to sing. Two years of singing Schumann and Bizet at the New England Conservatory didn't prepare me for Tom Sawyer's country trip down the Mississippi. I settled on "Amazing Grace." I didn't have the sheet music, but I'd sung it in my hometown church many times. I'd do it a cappella and give it a country twang. Plus, one verse was exactly 8 bars. Perfect!

Stanley Soble and the pianist were the only people in the room – both white guys with grey beards. I tried to be delightful as I stepped into the room, but nobody cracked a smile. Normally that would throw me off, but this time their somber faces didn't faze me. I stepped to the center of the room in front of stone-faced Stanley and started to sing.

"Amazing Grace, how sweet the sound... "

BOOM went the bass note on the piano. The pianist perfectly entered my song. He made the piano sound like an orchestra! My voice rode the wave of his heartfelt accompaniment. *Crescendo...diminuendo...*eight bars of "Amazing Grace" were suddenly a journey through time. We felt each other. We lived each moment, each note, each phrase. The song had a beginning, middle, and end. It was eight measures of *MAGIC*!

And then it was done. I glanced at the guys. They had a little laugh together. I giggled politely, said thank you, and left. I went home and tried not to think about it too much.

The next day I got a callback – for a Broadway show!

(Oh my God! Hallelujah! The director, Des McAnuff, is seeing me for Girl #3! Casting even sent me a scene to read for the leading lady! Oh joy! Oh rapture!)

And then...pure panic set in.

I'd heard that when you get a callback, you should sing what you sang at the original audition. There was a reason they liked that song choice. Sing it again for the team.

(Oh no! How can I sing "Amazing Grace" a cappella again? How could I possibly repeat the magic that happened at my audition? What if I start in another key? Would the pianist still magically come in? What if he doesn't and my a cappella version sucks? Besides, singing an easy song like "Amazing Grace" can't be enough for a big director like Des McAnuff!)

I loved Joan Baez's version of "Forever Young" by Bob Dylan. I got the sheet music and tried to make it sound good. Then I stumbled through the dialogue with my actor roommate Marty. Little voices of doubt kept rearing their heads. *(Who am I kidding? I don't know what I'm doing. They're gonna think I'm a fraud.)*

At the callback there was a room full of people behind the desk, and smack dab in the middle – Des McAnuff. After a few hellos, I sang my song. I tried to make it special. My song ended.

Suddenly, Des launched into his own Bob Dylan impersonation of "Forever Young." I smiled along like I thought he was funny. *(Oh my, this can't be good.)* Then I read the scene with Stanley Soble. The stage direction said to kiss Huck Finn, so I kissed Stanley on the cheek. *(Is it okay to kiss the casting director?)* I left the room deflated.

I didn't get the part. It was clear. I didn't know what the heck I was doing or who I was as a singer. Disappointment loomed.

* * *

I kept on auditioning every chance I could get. Well, that's the minimum a Broadway-singer-wanna-be *must* do. It's an important part of the job, even when you have a "job." You see, I had climbed the ladder at the Light Opera of Manhattan from chorus girl to leading lady tripling my pay to $105 a week. (Thank goodness for my part-time secretarial job.) I was singing the title character in the operettas *The Merry Widow* and *Naughty Marietta*, and the leading ingénue in many Gilbert & Sullivan classics like *HMS Pinafore* and *Iolanthe*.

I took a couple of months off from LOOM because my auditioning had finally paid off. I got into Actors' Equity (I'm a pro!) in a local dinner theater production of Maury Yeston's *Nine*. It was quite a production, peppered with Broadway starlets.

I was thrilled being cast as an "Italian" in the chorus under the baton of the future musical supervisor to Andrew Lloyd Webber, Kristen Blodgette.

My actor roommate Marty came to see me in the show. I couldn't wait for his feedback of my stellar chorus girl performance singing high C's and strutting my stuff in beautiful costumes.

"How did you like it?"

"You were good."

"Good? Was there something I could have done better?"

"Well, remember when you and the other ladies were pretending to get dressed?"

"Sure."

"You had a lot of energy touching up and down your dress – but that's not acting."

"What is acting?"

"You want to actually touch your dress – know you are touching your dress – don't pretend to touch your dress. Acting is being true."

"Oh."

I thought about what Marty had said. I decided to hire several Broadway vocal coaches to help me improve my acting skills. "Mary, be more like the character." "Be sad!" "Be happy!" "Be young!" "Be bold!" I would give them a sad, happy, young, and bold face – but even I could tell, it wasn't "true."

It was time to find a real acting class.

Finding Susan Batson

I began my search by meeting a renowned acting teacher. In the pre-screen interview he asked me about my acting experience. I told him proudly that I was the leading lady in repertory off-Broadway. He said that I couldn't be in a show *at all* if I wanted to take his class. I didn't sign up.

Then I found a workshop that was performing scenes from Chekov's *The Seagull*.

(Why not?) I jumped into the course! The play was triple cast, and I was one of the Mashas paired with an actor to do a scene.

I was standing on the stage in my A-line skirt and stylin' black leotard with one long sleeve and one naked arm. (I must have gone to dance class that day.) My partner and I began the scene. I got about seven words out before the short director leapt up onto the stage, totally disgusted.

"That was just awful. And Mary, why did you wear this for Masha? It's not helping the character at all."

The director tugged at the front of my leotard. Without warning, my breast popped out in front of his face! Flustered and bright red, the little director cowered away. I carefully pulled up my top, made a nonchalant face and tried not to dissolve. (I'm an actor, goddammit!)

He regrouped with a gulp. "Okay, let's try it again. Now Mary, you are to say the line and do something *disgusting* to your partner." I took a breath, said my line, and in one swift motion pulled down my leotard and exposed my breast again. The class swooned. I re-covered, recovered, and went on with the scene.

After class, one of the most talented actresses there came up to me. "You need to study with Susan Batson."

"Really? Who's that?"

"An amazing acting teacher."

"Why should I study with her?"

"Because of the way you handled yourself today. You have something special. Study with Susan. Trust me."

Acting Class

I didn't even think to tell Susan Batson that I was a singer, starring off-Broadway every night (and she didn't ask). I was a beginner. I was there to learn.

I went to class three days a week. Every lesson, Susan assigned us a different exercise. If Susan said, "You got the job!" life was good. My life sucked.

"Mary, you're shut down."

"You're stuck."

"Trust."

I knew Susan was right, but I had no idea how to fix it.

One day Susan told us to *Visit your father in the hospital*. The other students had tears streaming down their faces. Me? Dry-as-a-bone.

Weeks later during a *Confrontation Exercise*, I was so disconnected from my anger that Susan had me go around the room, stand in front of each student and say, "Fuck you!" I was as embarrassed as they were delighted.

Next class Susan announced, "Our business is competitive. Today I'll put you on stage to do an "Everyday Activity" that you think *you* do the best. *Something* that you do *every* day. Nobody else in the world does this activity as well as you. You'll go in groups of three."

My first thought was to floss. I am the best flosser in the world.

One actress cooked, another got dressed, one read a magazine, a guy combed his hair. A few got the job – a few didn't.

Susan called my group to the stage. As I walked to my spot, I had an epiphany. *(I'm playing "Naughty Marietta" every night. I practice singing every day. I'll sing scales!)* I took my place and sang my soprano vocalize with extended octaves. Up and down the scale I went. I saw Susan in the corner of my eye. She was awestruck.

As Murphy's Law would have it, the other two actresses chose singing as their activity too. *(Dammit. What are the odds? I better make this more interesting!)* I bagged the singing and jumped into practicing scenes from *Naughty Marietta*. Susan stopped the exercise.

"Mary...so...you're a singer."

"Yes." Susan just looked at me.

"Obviously singing scales is an activity you do every day. There was something so honest about it. I couldn't take my eyes off you. When you changed to the scene – that was not interesting. But those scales!" I smiled from ear to ear. Thank God I didn't floss.

From then on Susan knew who I was. I was beginning to know, too.

SING

Private Lesson

I scheduled my first private lesson with Susan. She sat me in a chair directly across from her. I had no idea what to expect.

"How was your weekend?" Susan asked warmly.

"I went to a wedding. A dear friend of mine just got married. I was asked to sing at the ceremony, which was really special — but I knew one of the groomsmen. He was my boyfriend for like two months. We just broke up last week. Ugh. There he was across the way. You know how it is when a guy knows you're there, but he doesn't acknowledge you? He didn't even shoot me a glance. He was laughing really loudly and flirting with the pretty bridesmaids. He knew I was in earshot."

"Did you go anywhere to get away from him?" Susan inquired.

"Yes."

"Where?"

"The bathroom."

"What do you remember about the bathroom?"

"I stood in front of the mirror."

"What were you doing?"

"Looking at myself."

"What was the sensation?"

(What was the sensation?) Nothing came to me.

"How did you feel?" Susan asked again.

I had no words. It felt like an hour went by.

"What are you aware of?"

Finally...finally...a word came into my mind. But dare I say it?

...

"Lonely."

"Yesssssssssssssssssss!!!!!!!!!"

Susan ran a victory lap around the studio! My eyes were like saucers looking at her have a *party* for my loneliness. I mean, she was actually celebrating my pain!

And then it hit me...that's what's missing! My painful feelings! I was always told to just "be happy and smile," but I can have painful feelings? To say "I'm lonely" is allowed?

Susan unlocked my truth. For the first time, I understood that my loneliness was actually an *asset* to my life. It was a jewel I could bring to my artist. A truth I could embrace for any character. A depth I could give to my work. Me, as I am, *all of me,* was the real work.

> "Mary, this is it," Susan said. "All feelings are required. When you are able to have your feelings completely free, you will then be able to connect those feelings with your voice. It's called the Need."

NEED

4. Emotional Life Side

NEED – Emotions

The Goal: To learn how to access your deep emotions and make art by singing through them. These deep emotions are called the Need.

Why This Is Important: When you "sing through" your Need, a voice emerges that has something utterly magical about it. It becomes a sound that nobody can teach you how to create. You see, your voice is not just the result of the quality of your vocal cords or the shape of your air pockets. Your voice is also the expression of a lifetime of experience filled with pain, joy, fear, triumph, hope, and all the other elements of the human experience. And believe it or not, with some practice, those who have never been able to carry a tune, discover that they can suddenly sing on pitch. It's a miracle.

What Needs To Change: You must stop *pretending* to feel when singing a song, and to instead actually feel and trust yourself.

MYTH: *You can't sing at your best if you get emotional, and you have no chance of singing well if you start to cry. Your job is to evoke emotions from the audience – not to feel them yourself.*

If I had succumbed to this Myth, I never would have found my own voice, or had a Broadway career. There is a craft to connect your deep emotions with your voice. Great actors have been doing this craft ever since Stanislavski arrived on the acting scene – but you don't have to be a professional actor to access your emotions. Do you sing in the car, weeping to your favorite Adele song when no one is listening? Does it feel good, and you think you actually sound pretty good?

You are already on the right path.

SINGING WITH EMOTIONS

You have arrived at the element that saved my singing career and saved my life — the Need. Studying classical voice at Stanford University and the New England Conservatory were paramount for my education, both as a performer and teacher. But something was missing — connecting my emotions with my voice.

It's not so easy to wave a magic wand, feel all of your emotions, trust yourself, and sing through those emotions — at least it wasn't easy for me. Even after my private lesson with Susan Batson, I remember standing alone in the corner of my New York apartment pointing to my stomach and demanding, "Open! Open! Open!" But the body and the emotions have their own timeline.

Each of us has a life full of stories. In those stories lie particular moments we don't want to remember — ever. We'd rather lock those painful memories away and move on. The poignant and difficult part of being human is that those are the memories that must be exposed and felt in order to be truly liberated. And when you are liberated, you are able to sing through your emotions. Or is it when you are able to sing through your emotions, you are liberated? As life goes, both may be true at the same time.

I continued working in acting class with Susan Batson on the Need three times a week for months on end. My emotions were stuck. I had to do the work. I had to go to the origin of the pain. Remember it. Feel it. And release it through song. I have always felt so lucky to be a singer — it's actually my *responsibility* to do this work. The happy result was that it not only helped me become a better singer, but it also helped heal those wounds at the source.

It became clear to me that I had to do some excavation of my childhood so I could finally meet and understand the emotions that were hiding. So, I did.

Me & My Dad

Growing up, Dad was my hero. He was the most charming, loving, and brilliant man I knew — and he loved to sing.

Singing songs was a prerequisite in my family, and from the age of three I couldn't get enough. Sunday mornings we'd gather on my parent's king-size bed. Under the sheets lying on his back, Dad would bend his knees into a blanket-covered mountain-top. One at a time, we kids would sit on top of the kneecap peak. The rule was we had to *sing a song at the top of our lungs* — and then, without warning, Dad's knees would drop, and we'd all dissolve into hysterical laughter. I loved every minute of it.

Many weekends, Dad sat me and my three brothers around a reel-to-reel tape recorder. He'd interview us and then we'd sing. We'd belt out in perfect harmony the old-time hits of the '20's: "If You Knew Suzie," "I Had a Dream Dear," and "Barney Google." My brothers were terrific singers, but Dad saw a star quality in me. He thought I had the potential to be like one of those original Broadway belters: Ethel Merman, Judy Garland, and Mary Martin. Daddy gave me my own one-on-one sessions too.

Miraculously I discovered those tapes in a box in the attic many years later.

"Oh, sure honey..." The microphone caught Dad's voice as he flipped on the recorder. "Now, today is October...the uh, October 7th...and it's quite a windy day this afternoon, isn't it? What did we do today? Hardly anything."

"Hardly go swimming too."

"No, we didn't, did we?"

"Well, we better."

"Oh, maybe later."

"Alright."

"Now — what is your name?"

"Mary."

"Mary what?"

"S--trakin."

"How old are you, Mary?"

"Can you tell me again?" little Mary whispered.

"You're three and a half."

"Three and a half."

"Now — are we going to sing a song?"

"Yeah."

"What?"

"I Wanna Girl Just Like the Girl That Married Dear Ol' Dad."

"Ok. Now let's see...I think that if we press this button and stop for a minute, we'll hold this...just a second here..."

NEED

Dad turned off the machine. "Here honey, take the mic." I had seen other singers hold a mic, so I brought it up to my mouth like a pro. Dad leaned in and adjusted it with his nimble fingers. "Just like that," he said, and set the little ukulele on his knee.

We had sung the song many times before, but never in front of all that big machinery. Dad flipped the switch back on.

"Ready?"

"Yeah," I smiled. Dad plucked the ukulele intro. *"I wanna girl JUST like the girl that MARRIED dear old DAD!"* I belted it out LOUD like Dad had taught me, and he sang along. I remember thinking, *(Shouldn't this microphone be making my voice really loud?)* I didn't know the mic was only recording my voice onto the tape. I screamed even louder. *"IIIIII wanna girl JUUUST like the girl that..."* (Nothing got louder, but I didn't care!)

"BRING IT HOME, MARY! BRING IT HOME!"

"MAAAARIED dear old DAAAAAAAAAD!

"Mary, that was terrific!" I glowed as my fearless leader, Daddy, praised me.

* * *

When I was six years old, once again we all gathered on my parent's king-size bed – but this time for a family meeting. Dad announced that he could only come home on weekends. He had to travel for work. I remember thinking, *(Okay, I can handle this...I'll be a good girl. I will only see Daddy on weekends, and that will be okay.)*

Little did we know – weekends would turn into months, even a year went by without seeing our father. The truth? Dad was in the midst of saving the failing family business, all the while his marriage was falling apart.

From the ages of six to thirteen, I'd often stand in my parent's bedroom looking in the big mirror at myself. I wasn't really looking – just listening. A few feet away, locked in the bathroom I'd hear my mother, alone, sobbing her eyes out. I'd stand there, holding my breath, swallowing back the pain. I felt helpless, my stomach churning, my insides eating me up. There were times I thought I could feel my heart actually breaking. Meanwhile – not a tear in sight. I was dry-as-a-bone. Maybe if I didn't cry, it wasn't really happening.

Don't Clean Up
Acting Class

Even though I was 100% committed to Susan Batson's acting workshops and private lessons, I still couldn't cry in class. I went to therapy in hopes of fixing my dry-as-a-bone problem. Let me tell you, it helped. There I'd sit, in the corner of Susan's classroom, sobbing my eyes out. I had no idea *what* I was crying about, but I was crying. This day was no different.

"What do I do, Susan?" I pleaded.

"Don't clean up, Mary. Cry. Keep crying. It's your turn, by the way." I stayed in the pain and took my place in front of the class. "Now...go back to the worst day of your life." *(Oh my God. Really? The worst day? I can't remember the worst day!)*

And then like magic – a scene came to my mind. I was thirteen years old, seeing a U-Haul truck in the driveway through my bedroom window. Nobody could see me. I was numb. Dad had just arrived to get his furniture. The divorce was final. My brother Robbie was helping Mom and Dad divide the furniture and load the truck since they weren't getting along. I heard loud noises – furniture dragging, truck engine revving. Dad was yelling orders at my brother as if he was the bullet boy in a war. "Rob! Rob!"

"And now sing." Susan said.

"I can't!" I sobbed.

"You must! Your instrument is opening up. This isn't therapy. We're not trying to fix your feelings. We're *using* them. It's uncontrollable now, but with practice, your instrument will be clear, and you will be the vessel. Don't clean up!" I thought she was mad at me. I started weeping through my song.

"It had to be you, it had to be you, I wandered around and finally found that somebody who..."

The numb good girl evaporated. There I was at the window, looking at Daddy steering the truck up the driveway, leaving our family behind. I sobbed through every word. "I'm crying! I can't sing!"

"Don't clean up, Mary!" Susan yelled. "Speak through it! SING THROUGH IT!"

"For nobody else gave me a thrill, with all your faults, I love you still..."

I was shaking. I was reaching to Daddy. I never told him, "Don't go! Stay with me!" Now I could tell him. I could sing it to him!

"It had to be you, wonderful you..."

Suddenly the sobbing united with my voice in one fell swoop. I could hear Daddy's reply, just like I was three years old in front of the microphone.

"BRING IT HOME, MARY! BRING IT HOME!"

"IT HAD TO BE YOU!"

My classmates applauded. Susan yelled, "YOU GOT THE JOB!"

HOW TO FIND YOUR NEED
An Unfulfilled Feeling

The Need is the element that is all emotions. It's not just a feeling, but an *unfulfilled* feeling. You could try and try to get rid of it, but it's not going anywhere. As human beings, we are always walking around in a Need – we're just not always aware of it. Or even worse, we hide these emotions from ourselves. They seem too painful to deal with.

You may be wondering – *How can I figure out what my personal Need is?*

Can you recall a time when you had that aching feeling inside – the feeling of the Need to be loved? – the Need for attention? – the Need for a hug? – the Need to be seen, heard, or understood? The sensation of those unfulfilled desires are all examples of a Need.

We carry these emotional sensations in our bodies our whole lives. When we're not getting the Need filled up, the deep desire is so intense. What was your Need when you were five years old? Ten? Fifteen? Do you feel a sensation of one of those Needs now? Which one? What are you aware of?

It is our job to have the Need present as we sing. The Need is only one of the ten elements of *The Revolutionary Send* – and all ten elements must be active to bring full mastery to your voice. If there was *only* Need, one could be called "self-indulgent." But *without* the Need, singing beautiful notes just isn't that interesting. The Need is the missing link.

> **An artist sees the blessing in every childhood hurt. The path to excavating, feeling, and triumphantly liberating those pains becomes the very food of artistic greatness. It's a way. A process. A journey. A doing. It brings your life closer to your full potential as an artist. Some paths are more treacherous than others, but all have worth. It's individually yours.**

HAPPY BIRTHDAY
Marilyn Monroe

We are now preparing the Need for the next and final chapter of *The Revolutionary Send,* Chapter Ten, when you will sing the iconic version of "Happy Birthday" by Marilyn Monroe – *Happy Birthday Mr. President.*

Here is our question – What is Marilyn Monroe's Need?

Marilyn Monroe's childhood and personal life have been well chronicled as painful, lonely, and complicated with feelings of abandonment. She has a plethora of Needs that could apply. But when I think of Marilyn Monroe singing "Happy Birthday" to President Kennedy, I can imagine her "Need for attention." As a girl who grew up never knowing who her father even was, it seems plausible that Marilyn Monroe desperately needed a man's attention. To get the attention from a man who some might call the most powerful man in the world – the President of the United States – must have been quite intoxicating indeed.

Let's choose for Marilyn Monroe – the "Need for attention."

In finding Marilyn Monroe's "Need for attention," you will be applying your personal "Need for attention" as you connect truthfully to this iconic version of "Happy Birthday."

Sense Memory Exercise
Need for Attention

To find *your* "Need for attention," I'll be taking you through a Sense Memory Exercise. Right now, think of a time when you needed a certain person's attention, but you didn't get it. It could be one of your parents, an unrequited love, or even the person you've been using so far, the person you'd "love to see today." Then, go back to that moment in time when you didn't get attention from this person. It could have been a moment from your childhood, a moment from many years ago, or some time more recently. Choose the *worst* moment with this person when you felt you weren't getting ANY attention from them. It might not have even been true, but if it felt true to *you,* that's the right choice. Even if it was just a fleeting moment, that's enough! Here we go!

EXERCISE TO FIND YOUR "NEED FOR ATTENTION"

GIVE IT A TRY!

SENSE MEMORY EXERCISE

Sit comfortably. Take a few easy breaths. Let the air enter the bottom of your lungs and notice your tummy releasing *out* on the inhale and falling on the exhale. As you breathe, be aware of your inner life and your emotions – whatever they may be. Let The Breath live as you experience this exercise. You can keep your eyes open or closed – as you please.

Go back to a time in your life when you were craving attention from this particular person, but you got NO attention. As you remember this *worst* moment, answer these questions to yourself:

1. How long ago was it when you needed attention from this person but got NO attention? When you were a child? Many years ago? Seven years ago? Last month? Yesterday?

2. What time of year was it – what season? Winter? Spring? Summer? Fall?

3. What time of day was it? Morning? Mid-day? Afternoon? Evening? Middle of the night?

4. *Where* were you? Inside? Outside? What specific place?

5. What do you remember about the *place* that you'll never forget? The window? The bed? The light? The ocean? The street lamp?

6. What were you wearing?

7. Who was the person you wanted attention from?

8. In that moment when you needed attention, what did the person *say* or *do* that you'll never forget as long as you live?

9. What did you *want* to say to that person, but you didn't?

10. Say it now!
    Yell it!
    Scream it!
    Get it OUT!
    Get it OUT!!!!!!!

The thing that you wanted to say but didn't is the PULSE of your Need. That is the trigger to connect you to your "Need for attention."

> ## WHAT ARE YOU AWARE OF?
>
> Did you yell what you wanted to say to the person? Is it the first time you've ever said something like that them? Doesn't it feel good?! Perhaps you'd never say that to your person in real life, but here you have permission! Even if you're shy and it's difficult to say the words, at least whisper the words! That is progress. To release the words and the emotions is the key. Did you cry? Don't clean up! Cry!

SINGING THROUGH TEARS

If tears come up when you are feeling the Need, just as Susan Batson said to me, *don't clean up! Speak and sing through it!* I'm often asked how to sing through tears. *What do you do if you get choked up and you can't sing?* The answer is – you keep practicing! To sing through your emotions is an artform. Have you seen Oscar award–winning actors crying and speaking at the same time in their movie scenes? They had to practice doing that. So do you. Whenever the emotions come up and you feel choked up, just keep speaking and singing through it, even if you sound like a frog. With time, you too will become the open vessel.

PREPARING HAPPY BIRTHDAY
Adding the Need

We are now going to set up your Fourth Wall to connect you to your "Need for attention" as you sing "Happy Birthday." This is *not* your final performance! This is a chance to practice *just* the one element of **Need** as you sing.

ADDING THREE POINTS

You already know how put your **Personalization** on the **center point** on your **Fourth Wall**. Now you're going to **add two more points** on your **Fourth Wall**.

- Find a **center point** on your Fourth Wall
- Find a second point a bit to the **right of center**
- Find a third point a bit to the **left of center**
- Don't pick a point too far right or left – Remember, *your eyes are the window to your soul,* and the audience needs to see your eyes

PERSON, PLACE, & DREAM

1. On the **center point**, put the **person** from whom you have a deep "Need for attention." What is their strongest physical feature? What is their strongest human quality?

2. On the **right point** of your Fourth Wall remember from the Sense Memory Exercise the **place**. What is it in the **place** you will never forget? Put that element of **place** on that **right point**.

3. On the **left point** of your Fourth Wall, put your **dream** with the person. What would it be like if your person gave you all of the attention you need? Where would you be? What would they do? Put that **dream** on the **left point**.

MARY'S PREPARATION

I will answer each of the above questions to give you an example of how to prepare your **Fourth Wall** for "Happy Birthday" using your "Need for attention."

For the worst moment in my life when I had the "Need for attention," I'll choose the day my father took away his half of the furniture from our home when my parent's divorce was final.

1. On the **center point** I'll put my father – (he was also the person I'd "love to see today"). His strongest physical feature is his face, and his strongest human quality is his generosity.

2. On the **right point** I'll put the thing in the **place** that I'll never forget: the truck outside my window driving away.

3. On the **left point** I'll put my **dream** with my father: My dream is to sit with my father and have a wonderful conversation with him as he tells me how proud he is of me.

SING YOUR SONG THREE TIMES – PERSON, PLACE, & DREAM

You will now sing "Happy Birthday" three times – one full time to your **person**, one full time to your **place**, and one full time to your **dream**. Choose the easiest key in your range. You can't do it wrong.

YOUR PREPARATION: Remember from the Sense Memory Exercise what your person said or did that you'll never forget as long as you live. What did you want to say to that person, but didn't? Say it out loud! Now you are in the PULSE of your "Need for attention."

MARY'S PREPARATION: The thing my father said or did was to drive away in the truck with all the furniture. The thing I wanted to say to him but didn't was "Don't go! Stay with me!" I'm now in the sensation of the "Need for attention."

HAPPY BIRTHDAY WITH THE "NEED FOR ATTENTION"

"PERSON" – CENTER POINT

- See your **person** on the **center point** of your **Fourth Wall**

- Take an easy inhale

- Sing through the sensation of your unfulfilled **"Need for attention"** directly to your person

---

Hap - py birth - day to you Hap - py birth - day to you Hap - py

birth - day dear Dad - dy Hap - py birth - day to you

WHAT ARE YOU AWARE OF?

Are you aware of the emotional sensation of your **"Need for attention?"** You are now connecting your emotions directly to your voice. Do not worry at all about the "sound" of your voice. Just speak and sing "Happy Birthday" right through your emotions.

"PLACE" – RIGHT POINT

- See on the **right point** of your **Fourth Wall** your **place** from the *worst day*

- Take an easy inhale

- Sing through the sensation of your unfulfilled **"Need for attention"** as you see your **place**

WHAT ARE YOU AWARE OF?

Are you aware of the **place** on the *worst day* of your "Need for attention?" Did emotions come up? Don't clean up! And don't worry about the "sound" of your voice. Keep speaking and singing through it!

"DREAM" – LEFT POINT

- See on the **left point** of your **Fourth Wall** your **dream** with the person

- Take an easy inhale

- Sing through the sensation of your unfulfilled **"Need for attention"** directly to your **dream** with the person

WHAT ARE YOU AWARE OF?

Are you aware of the **dream** with your person and your **"Need for attention?"** You don't want to "show" your emotions – instead, just *let* the Need live in your body. You are connecting to your intimacy.

INTIMACY = INTO – ME – SEE

As you see your **person**, **place,** and **dream** on the **Fourth Wall**, be brave enough to reveal your *intimacy*. Don't "show" your feelings. Let the emotions live in your body and sing through that sensation. As you reveal your vulnerable truth, you are stepping into your intimacy = INTO-ME-SEE.

This new way to *expose* your intimate self will touch the personal story of each audience member. Don't worry about the audience discovering something secret about your life. The audience is not interested in the intimate details of *your* story. They have come to find themselves in you.

Organize yourself... Please check off **Need**.

THE REVOLUTIONARY SEND

VOICE TECHNIQUE SIDE	EMOTIONAL LIFE SIDE
1. The Breath	1. Personalization
2. Support	2. Fourth Wall
3. Resonance	3. Sensory Condition
4. Floors	4. Need
5. Pyramid	**5. Action**

Congratulations! You have now gone through nine out of the ten elements of my method, *The Revolutionary Send!* It's time to sing through all nine elements and SEND them on the tenth and final element – **Action**, through Marilyn Monroe's version of "Happy Birthday." *Happy Birthday Mr. President.* Let's do this!

chapter ten

ACTION

MARILYN MONROE

Happy Birthday Mr. President

Marilyn Monroe ran onto the stage in quick tippy toe steps to sing "Happy Birthday" to President John Kennedy. She couldn't see him in the audience, so on her **Fourth Wall** she imagined President Kennedy's handsome face and felt his powerful presence – her **Personalization**. Marilyn Monroe had always had the "**Need** for attention." On this day, his 45th birthday, she would have loved for President Kennedy to have given *her* attention. (Maybe she wasn't even aware of this unfulfilled emotion.) She knew she could get attention by being a sex symbol, so Marilyn felt the *sensation of oil* all over her body. That **Sensory Condition** was always present for Marilyn – it made her feel sexy and alive. Marilyn took a **Breath**, then swung her bellybutton **Support** IN – and her voice started to resonate. "*Happy birthday to you*" – the **Resonance** tickled her face. She sang up the scale and up the **Floors** in the shape of a **Pyramid**, "*Happy biiiiirthday Mr. President...*" Marilyn *sent* her voice on the **Action**: "to seduce." Not only did Mr. President feel the seduction of her rendition of "Happy Birthday," but the whole audience swooned as if she was singing to each of them alone. "*Happy birthday...to... youuuu.*"

Of course, I never worked with Marilyn Monroe, but watching the video of that day, Marilyn embraced the elements of *The Revolutionary Send* as if she was my co-author.

ACTION

5. Emotional Life Side

ACTION – Send

The Goal: To learn how to take all ten elements of *The Revolutionary Send* and *send* them on an **Action** through your song. An **Action** is always a verb – as in "to charm," "to seduce," "to demand," "to fight," "to flatter," …

Why This Is Important: You must *send* your voice on an **Action** in order to be heard – and *share* your vulnerability – and *share* a true story. If not, the audience won't hear you, feel you, or understand you.

What Has To Change: It's now your job to choose the Action that will serve the story of your song – and live it truthfully.

FINDING THE ACTION

> **The Need is the propeller of human behavior. – Susan Batson**

Susan Batson taught me that *the Need is the propeller of human behavior* – meaning that our unfulfilled Need supplies the impulse of the Actions we take. We are all walking around in a Need – but we all make different choices of how to respond to that unfulfilled emotion operating. The Actions can range from a good healthy response to destructive ones.

For example, my personal Need is the "Need to be heard." My Action is to write this book so that you will hear everything about me and what I have to say (my Action: "to give my all"). My intention is to give you good information that will help you – so that's a good Action propelled by my "Need to be heard."

Examples of destructive Actions can be pointed out in the movie classic – psychological thriller, *Fatal Attraction* starring Glenn Close and Michael Douglas. (If you don't know this movie, it's a good one to study the connection between Need and Action.) Glenn Close's character Alex has a desperate "Need for attention," and sets her eyes on Dan, a married colleague played by Michael Douglas. Alex's first Action is "to seduce" Dan. It works, and they have an affair. Then, not getting the exclusive attention she's craving, Alex escalates her Action, from attempting suicide ("to cry for help"), to claiming she's pregnant with his baby ("to manipulate"), and eventually climaxing to the famous scene of Dan's wife finding the family pet rabbit in a pot of boiling water on their kitchen stove ("to kill"). These thriller movie scenes are examples of high-stake Actions – human behavior being propelled by the "Need for attention."

The Need is only emotion, but the Action drives the story forward. You can think of the Action in several ways:

1. The Action can be *contrary* to the Need
2. The Action can be a way to *hide* or *cover up* the Need
3. The Action can *distract* others from being aware of the Need

To find the overall Action of your song, we look to the Need for guidance. Here are some examples:

1. The "Need to be loved" – the Action: "to push love away"
2. The "Need to be important" – the Action: "to be bossy"
3. The "Need to be respected" – the Action: "to fight"

In Marilyn Monroe's life, she had a deep "Need for attention." That unfulfilled Need drove the behavior that made her an iconic sex symbol – like the Action "to seduce."

For Marilyn Monroe's version of *Happy Birthday Mr. President,* we have chosen the "Need for attention," and let's send on the Action "to seduce."

HAPPY BIRTHDAY MR. PRESIDENT

A la Marilyn Monroe

Now it's your turn to sing *Happy Birthday Mr. President* just like Marilyn Monroe did using *all* ten elements of *The Revolutionary Send*. We will be looking back on the tools and choices you made in the previous nine chapters and bring them to song. Here's a reminder of all ten elements of *The Revolutionary Send*:

THE REVOLUTIONARY SEND

VOICE TECHNIQUE SIDE	EMOTIONAL LIFE SIDE
1. **The Breath**	1. **Personalization**
2. **Support**	2. **Fourth Wall**
3. **Resonance**	3. **Sensory Condition**
4. **Floors**	4. **Need**
5. **Pyramid**	5. **Action**

SONG PREPARATION

As we step into your Song Preparation, be aware that this lesson can be used as a "blueprint" to help you prepare your songs in the future. Connecting the five voice technique elements *with* your emotional life and *sending* them on an Action is the key. Your hard work is paying off! Here we go!

Morning Routine

The Breath, Support, and Resonance

As we begin our preparation, let's first wake up your voice – but not just for today. For *every* day! Here I offer you a daily challenge in your personal morning routine to wake up **The Breath**, **Support**, and **Resonance** of your voice and body before you even begin your day. Though I promise – it won't be that challenging! Only one minute of your time.

What is your morning routine? You roll out of bed — and then what do you do? Have a cup of coffee? Brush your teeth? Comb your hair? Take a shower? Get dressed? Eat breakfast? There is probably a moment during your morning routine when you find yourself in front of a mirror, like when you're brushing your teeth or combing your hair. This is where the challenge begins. While standing in front of the mirror, just add this brief ritual to your daily routine. Give it a try it now:

1. The Breath

Stand in front of a mirror. As you see yourself in the mirror, be aware of your breathing and take an **Economical Breath**. Simply breathe through your nose and mouth at the same time and watch your tummy in the mirror release OUT with each inhale. (Don't let the air rise high into your chest around your clavicles.) You are a pro at this now, so you can enjoy the fact that you understand (without actually feeling it) that the phrenic nerve is sending a signal to your diaphragm. With every inhale, your diaphragm receives the signal, contracts, and drops down creating a vacuum in your lungs. Because the diaphragm pushes aside your organs as it descends, your tummy releases OUT as you inhale. Got it? Bravo!

2. Support

Now on the exhale, add your Super Bellybutton **Support** with an "Sssssss." Swing your bellybutton IN and watch in the mirror as your sternum freely bounces OUT with every exhale as you say "Ssssss." Repeat taking a **Silent Breath** and saying "Ssssss" with your bellybutton **Support** swinging IN a few times.

3. Resonance

Now instead of "Ssssss," on every exhale say "Hmmmmm," and chew. Feel the *sensation of vibration* around your mouth and cheeks. If you are somebody who is susceptible to vocal fry, this exercise is paramount to set in place your healthy **Resonance**. Do that a few times: Inhale with **The Breath**, swing your bellybutton **Support** IN, say "Hmmmmm," and chew. Feel the **Resonance**.

Just as you brush your teeth and comb your hair every morning, now you'll also wake up your voice and body, so it's aligned and ready for the day. Even without singing a note, you will be "practicing" throughout the day as you speak, efficiently connecting The Breath and Support with your Resonance — your voice.

Now you're ready for your day, *and* you're ready to continue your preparation for *Happy Birthday Mr. President*.

4. Need

Now that **The Breath**, **Support**, and **Resonance** are hooked up and ready to go — first thing's first, finding the **Need**. For Marilyn Monroe's version of *Happy Birthday Mr. President*, you want to go back to the time you had the "Need for attention." To do this, let's repeat the Sense Memory Exercise you just did in Chapter Nine. Every time you do this exercise, you may discover a deeper awareness of your **Need**.

SENSE MEMORY EXERCISE – "NEED FOR ATTENTION"

Sit comfortably. Take a few easy breaths. Let the air enter the bottom of your lungs and notice your tummy releasing *out* on the inhale and falling on the exhale. As you breathe, be aware of your inner life and your emotions — whatever they may be. Let The Breath live as you experience this exercise. You can keep your eyes open or closed — as you please.

Go back to a time in your life when you were craving attention from this particular person, but you got NO attention. As you remember this *worst* moment, answer these questions to yourself:

1. How long ago was it when you needed attention from this person but got NO attention? When you were a child? Many years ago? Seven years ago? Last month? Yesterday?

2. What time of year was it — what season? Winter? Spring? Summer? Fall?

3. What time of day was it? Morning? Mid-day? Afternoon? Evening? Middle of the night?

4. *Where* were you? Inside? Outside? What specific place?

5. What do you remember about the *place* that you'll never forget? The window? The bed? The light? The ocean? The street lamp?

6. What were you wearing?

7. Who was the person you wanted attention from?

8. In that moment when you needed attention, what did the person *say* or do that you'll never forget as long as you live?

9. What did you *want* to say to that person, but you didn't?

10. Say it now!
    Yell it!
    Scream it!
    Get it OUT!
    Get it OUT!!!!!!!

The thing that you wanted to say but didn't is the PULSE of your Need. That is the trigger to connect you to your "Need for attention."

You've got it? Please stay in the "Need for attention" during this whole preparation. It's the perfect way to practice feeling the sensation of the "Need for attention" so that it will be present when it's time for your performance. Remember, the Need is just an emotional *sensation*. This unfulfilled emotion is always present during the song. You don't want to "show" the emotion – just drop into your "Need for attention," and trust that it's there.

5. Personalization

Having experienced again the Sense Memory Exercise from Chapter Nine, you are now aware of your **Parallel Situation** of Marilyn Monroe's version of *Happy Birthday Mr. President*. It's time to choose your specific **person**, **place**, and **dream**:

a) **Person**: Who is *your* Mr. President, the person you crave attention from? What is their strongest physical feature and their strongest human quality?

b) **Place**: *Where* were you on the worst day when you felt the "Need for attention?" What detail about the place where you *didn't* get attention will you never forget? Was it a window? The bed? The ocean? The street lamp?

c) **Dream**: What is your dream with the person? What would it be like if you got *all* the attention you wanted from this person? What would you be doing together?

6. **Fourth Wall**

Your **person**, **place**, and **dream** are ready to be put up on your Fourth Wall. Stand and find a central point, right point, and left point on your Fourth Wall. Think of the **person** you want attention from. On your center point, theatrically "see" the strongest physical feature of your person and "feel" their strongest human quality. On your right point, put the strongest thing in the **place** where your Need was unfulfilled. And then on your left point, put your **dream** with the person. If you could receive the attention you crave from your person, what would that dream be?

Because "Happy Birthday" is not a very long song, you will only be singing directly to your **person** on the center point in the final exercise. But keep the **place** and **dream** on the other two points. This way, your entire **Fourth Wall** will cocoon you in the privacy of your unfulfilled "Need for attention." Those details of **place** and **dream** help you stay in the pain of the *worst* day when you had *no* attention, and the beautiful dream of what could be. This specific and truthful work will bring your voice to a new level. As the adage goes, *"God is in the details."*

7. **Sensory Condition**

Just like Marilyn Monroe, feel the *sensation of oil* all over your body. To practice this sensation, you can rub baby oil all over your body. Don't forget your face, lips, and forehead (please don't get baby oil in your eyes or accidentally ingest any). In addition to the oil, let's add the **Sensory Condition** of stepping into the "femme fatale" character of Marilyn Monroe, or as the "stud" character of Elvis Presley. Move your mouth and feel the *sensation of oil* while taking on your preferred character. You'll notice in the lyrics of the song I added the option of singing to "Mister President" or "Madame President." Feel free to use whatever gender suites you. You're now in the "Need for attention," and you feel the *sensation of oil* all over your body. Your mouth is moving like Marilyn Monroe or Elvis Presley.

8. Floors

As you see your person on the center point of your Fourth Wall, start humming the melody of "Happy Birthday" and chew. Be aware of the **Floors** around your mouth, as the humming vibration tickles your face in the Front Passage resonators.

9. Pyramid

As you approach the famous octave leap in "Happy Birthday," continue humming. As you hum up the octave, be sure to increase the pressure of your bellybutton **Support**. It zips IN as you start from the **Floors** around your mouth and then jump up to the **Floors** around your eyes. Be aware of the shape of the **Pyramid** as you hum up and down the melody of "Happy Birthday."

10. Action

You are ready! It's time to send all nine elements of *The Revolutionary Send* through the final element – **Action**. Try to find a stage with an audience: Like sing for your mom in the kitchen, or invite your neighbors and sing for them on your back porch. Or if no one is home, sing for your dog. And if you don't have a dog, this time just set it up "as if" you had an audience. All good! Remember, your Action for *Happy Birthday Mister/Madame President* is – (drum roll) – **"to seduce."** This action can certainly be sexy and sensual, but if your person doesn't qualify for romantic love (like a family member), "to seduce" can also just be playful and fun. When you see your specific person, the Action "to seduce" will live in its truth – that is perfect. Here we go!

HAPPY BIRTHDAY MISTER/MADAME PRESIDENT

Stepping onto the stage, you theatrically "see" your Mister/Madame President on the center point of your **Fourth Wall**. You imagine their strongest physical feature and feel their strongest human quality – your **Personalization**. On this day, your "**Need** for attention" from Mister/Madame President is so strong. You feel the *sensation of oil* all over your body, and your mouth moves sensually like Marilyn Monroe or Elvis Presley. The **Sensory Condition** makes you feel courageous, vibrant, and alive. You take a **Silent Breath**, and then swing your bellybutton **Support** IN – your voice starts to resonate. "*Happy birthday to you*" – the **Resonance** tickles your face. You sing up the octave leap and up the **Floors** in the shape of a **Pyramid**, "*Happy biiiiirthday Mister/Madame President...*" You *send* your voice on the **Action**: "to seduce." Not only does the President feel the seduction of your rendition of "Happy Birthday," but the whole audience swoons as if you were singing to each of them alone. "*Happy birthday...to... youuuu.*"

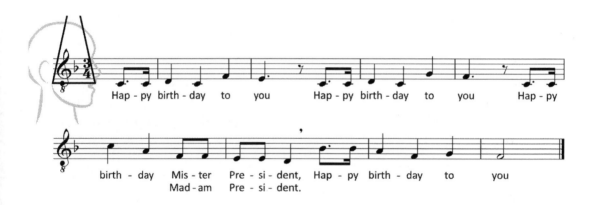

Hap - py birth - day to you Hap - py birth - day to you Hap - py

birth - day Mis - ter Pre - si - dent, Hap - py birth - day to you
Mad - am Pre - si - dent.

WHAT ARE YOU AWARE OF?

How was your journey of connecting all ten elements of *The Revolutionary Send* singing *Happy Birthday Mr. President*? Did you stay private with your **Personalization** on your **Fourth Wall**? Did you feel the *sensation of oil* and connect to the **Sensory Condition** character of Marilyn Monroe or Elvis Presley? Was your "Need for attention" present? Remember, the **Need** is just an emotional sensation. You don't want to *show* your feelings. Just trust that the emotion is living in your body. That is enough. How did **The Breath**, **Support**, and **Resonance** go as you sang the octave leap up the **Floors** through the shape of the **Pyramid**? And finally, did you *send* your voice on the **Action**, "to seduce?" Did you have fun being playful and seducing your person?

YOU HAVE JUST COMPLETED
THE REVOLUTIONARY SEND!
BRAVO!

Congratulations! You have successfully completed my program, *The Revolutionary Send*! I'm so honored that you are on this journey with me. I hope you enjoy putting these ten elements into practice as you keep growing as a singer and as a human being.

Up next you'll find the *The Vocal Exercises All In One Place* as well as *The Healing Vocal Exercise*. Keep these in your back pocket. They are ready for you when you need them.

As for the future, the ten elements of my method, *The Revolutionary Send,* are at the core of all the information yet to come, but there's much more. In my next offering, Volume II, *SING – Stylings & Interpretation,* you'll venture on to quite advanced technical and acting material – including singing in all different styles (from Classical to Broadway to Pop), a deep dive into song preparation and interpretation, and challenging vocal exercises. Please don't be shy in moving forward, even if you call yourself a beginner. Singing is your birthright. These tools are there for you. Let's SING!

The
Vocal
Exercises

introduction

Welcome to **PART II – The Vocal Exercises**. I want you to have a warm-up that you can go to every day. Here we go!

First up in Chapter Eleven are all the exercises you've done throughout the book. They are there for you to practice with, but without the stories and extra information, so you can access them quickly and easily. If you want to go back for a full review, the corresponding chapters are always waiting for you any time.

I've organized the exercises in a particular order so you can choose a one-minute exercise – ten-minute warmup – twenty-minute warmup, and so on – whatever works for you in your schedule. I have personally found that doing just a couple of exercises daily helps keep the body/mind/emotions connection stay in shape and assure a healthy voice.

If you'd like to do a longer warmup, I suggest a schedule that my flute teacher, Merrill Jordan, gave me when I was a teenager:

- Two thirty-minute sessions a day

Mr. Jordan said that since the flute is a wind instrument, it's best to practice in shorter sessions rather than hours in a row (like pianists often do). As singers our body is also a kind of wind instrument, so I think it's a wonderful suggestion if it resonates with you. You never want to exhaust your voice singing too many vocal exercises before working on repertoire or performing. As the adage says, *don't leave your voice in the practice room.*

In Chapter Twelve you'll find The Healing Vocal Exercise. I discovered this exercise from Dr. Ruth Epstein in the UK who encouraged me to share my personal version of it. I was thrilled to discover this exercise because it incorporates the "Ssssss," tongue trills, and lip trills – both voiced and unvoiced – with a big emphasis on correct Breath and Support. I've found it to be a remarkable tool for both waking up the voice and for cooling down the voice at the end of the day. When

Kerry Washington was performing eight shows a week on Broadway in the play *American Son*, it was important to not overwork Kerry's voice, but still make sure she was technically hooked up and *ready* for the play. We used this exercise often for her pre-show warmup. Kerry loved it. Some of my students end their day with this exercise for vocal restoration after a lot of singing or talking. For me, it's a little miracle in your back pocket.

chapter eleven

THE VOCAL EXERCISES
ALL IN ONE PLACE

From here on in, I encourage you to keep *The Revolutionary Send* on hand. Now that you understand the ten elements, they will serve you well as you practice with them today and for years to come.

THE REVOLUTIONARY SEND	
VOICE TECHNIQUE SIDE	**EMOTIONAL LIFE SIDE**
1. The Breath	1. Personalization
2. Support	2. Fourth Wall
3. Resonance	3. Sensory Condition
4. Floors	4. Need
5. Pyramid	5. Action

MORNING ROUTINE

The Breath, Support, & Resonance

Let's make the Morning Routine from Chapter Ten a staple in your life — it only requires one minute of your time.

As you're preparing for your day, find a moment when you're standing in front of a mirror, and add this brief but powerful ritual to your daily routine.

1. **The Breath**

   As you see yourself in the mirror, take an **Economical Breath**. Simply breathe through your nose and mouth at the same time silently and watch your tummy in the mirror release OUT with each inhale. (Don't let the air rise high into your chest around your clavicles.)

2. **Support**

   Now on the exhale, add your Super Bellybutton **Support** with an "Sssssss." Swing your bellybutton IN and watch in the mirror as your sternum freely bounces OUT with every "Sssss" exhale. Do numbers 1 and 2 a few times.

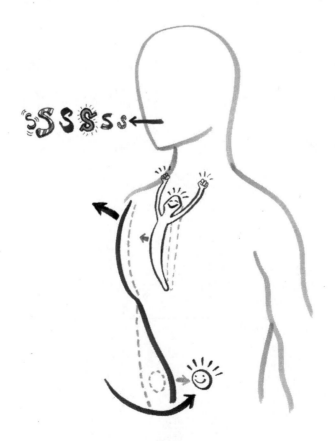

SING

3. Resonance

Now instead of "Ssssss," on every exhale say "Hmmmmm" and chew. Feel the *sensation of vibration* around your mouth and cheeks in the Front Passage. If you're somebody who is susceptible to vocal fry, this exercise is paramount to find your healthy **Resonance**. Do that a few times: Inhale with the **Silent Breath**, swing your bellybutton IN for your **Support**, and say "Hmmmmm" and chew. Now add the **Sensory Condition** of sunshine, and say "Hmmmmm" again through that sensation. Beautiful!

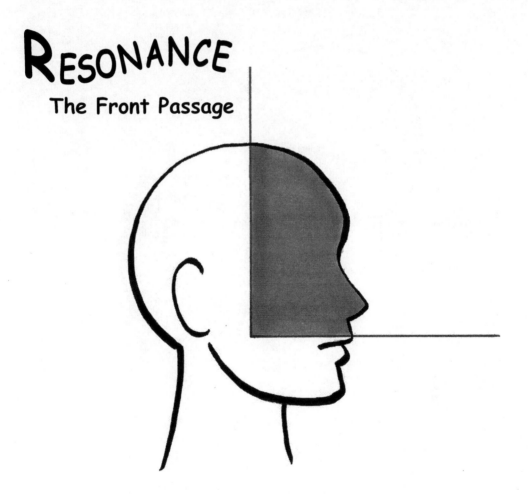

RESONANCE
The Front Passage

You are now ready for your day!

QUICK CHECK – HAND ON CHEEKS

SPEAKING – HANDS ON CHEEKS

- Put your hands ON your cheeks

- Take an easy **inhale**

- Bounce the bellybutton Support IN for each staccato syllable and speak [mi ' me ' ma ' mo ' mu'] while pulling your hands AWAY from your cheeks on each syllable

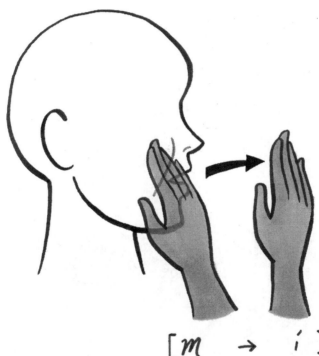

$$[m \rightarrow i]$$
$$[m \rightarrow \varepsilon]$$
$$[m \rightarrow a]$$
$$[m \rightarrow o]$$
$$[m \rightarrow u]$$

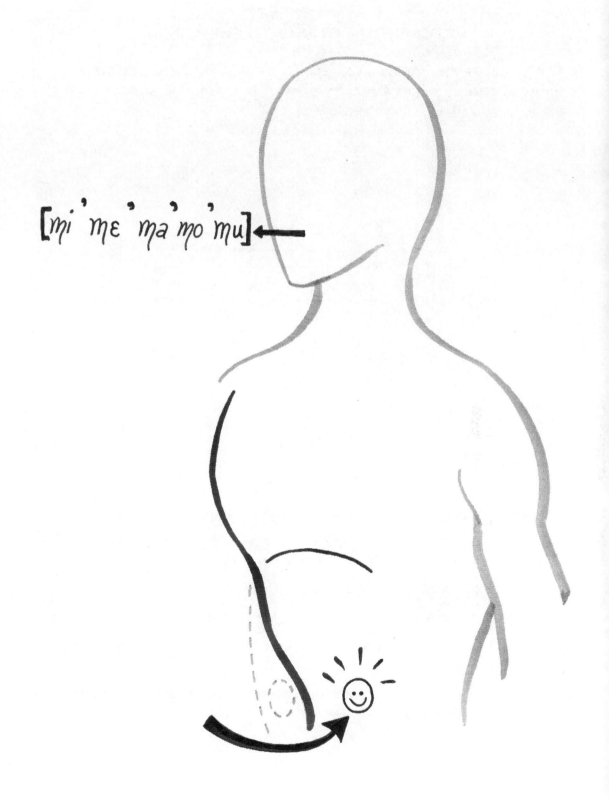

THE VOCAL EXERCISES ALL IN ONE PLACE

ADD PITCH – STACCATO EXERCISE

Choose a pitch that is around your speaking voice. The picture below shows the musical note middle C, which for most is around the speaking voice. (Men, your voice rings an octave lower.)

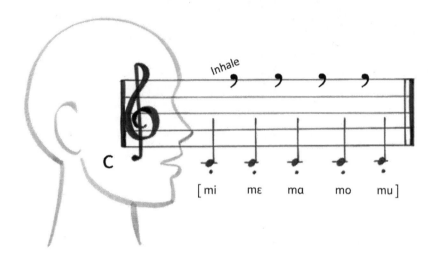

[mi   mɛ   ma   mo   mu]

GIVE IT A TRY!

- See the person you would love to see today, your **Personalization**, on the central point of your **Fourth Wall** – feel your **Need** for that person

- Take a **Silent Breath** and let your bellybutton **Support** bounce IN for each staccato interval singing [**mi ' me ' ma ' mo ' mu'**]

- Bounce the bellybutton **Support** IN with each staccato note

- At the same time, add a little bouncing knee bend for each staccato note

- Release your head side to side through the **Sensory Condition** of sunshine with each staccato note

- SEND the Staccato Exercise to your **Personalization** the **Fourth Wall** with the **Action** of "Hello! Greetings!"

LEGATO EXERCISE ASCENDING

LEGATO EXERCISE [mi – me – ma – mo – mu]

- See the person you would love to see today, your **Personalization**, on the central point of your **Fourth Wall** – feel your **Need** for that person

- Take an easy **Silent Breath** through your nose and mouth at the same time

- Initiate the **Support** from your bellybutton – moving IN

- As your bellybutton moves IN, SEND out the syllables connecting smoothly in a row through the [m] **Resonance [mi – me – ma – mo – mu]**

- Bring your arm up slowly feeling the **Sensory Condition** of OIL on your face and arms, and **REACH** to your person as you sing **[mi – me – ma – mo – mu]**

- Repeat: As you **REACH** to your person, relax your tongue so the tip of the tongue touches your bottom teeth, and move and your jaw side to side in the sensation of OIL as you sing **[mi – me – ma – mo – mu]**

- Feel the vibration in your **Front Passage Resonators** around your mouth as you SEND the Legato Exercise to your person on the **Action** "to seduce," moving your jaw side to side in the sensation of OIL

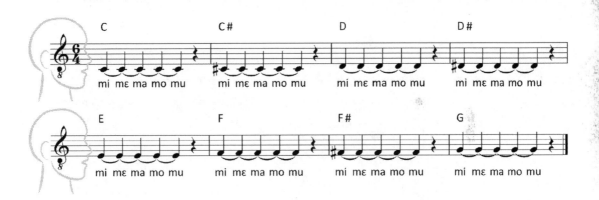

LEGATO EXERCISE DESCENDING

Now repeat as you descend the scale with the Legato Exercise

- See the person you would love to see today, your **Personalization**, on the central point of your **Fourth Wall** – feel your **Need** for that person

- Take an easy **Silent Breath** through your nose and mouth at the same time

- Initiate the **Support** from your bellybutton – moving IN

- As your bellybutton moves IN, SEND out the syllables connecting smoothly in a row through the [m] **Resonance [mi – me – ma – mo – mu]**

- Bring your arm up slowly feeling the sensation of OIL on your face and arms, and **REACH** to your person as you sing **[mi – me – ma – mo – mu]** through the **Action** "to seduce"

- Repeat: As you REACH to your person, relax your tongue so the tip of the tongue touches your bottom teeth, and move and your jaw side to side in the **Sensory Condition** of OIL as you sing **[mi – me – ma – mo – mu]** through the **Action** "to seduce"

- Feel the vibration in your **Front Passage Resonators** around your mouth as you SEND the Legato Exercise to your person on the **Action** "to seduce," moving your jaw side to side in the sensation of OIL

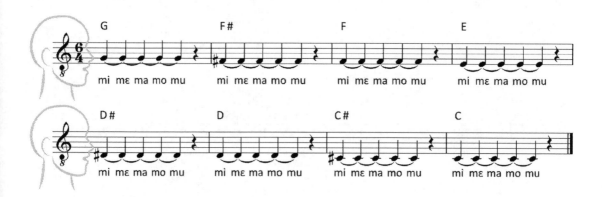

SLIDING EXERCISES UP AND DOWN AN OCTAVE

Sliding Hum Exercise – "Hmmmmm"

Say "Hmmmmm" sliding Up and Down the **Floors** of the **Front Passage** in the shape of a **Pyramid** in an octave interval.

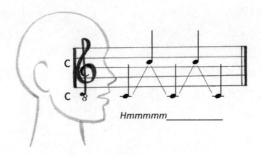

Sliding Tongue Trill Exercise – "Drrrrr"

Now say "Drrrrr" with **Tongue Trill** up and down the **Floors** in the shape of a **Pyramid** in an octave interval.

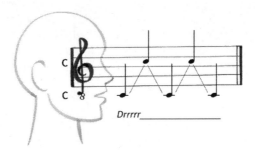

Sliding Lip Trill Exercise – "Brrrrr"

Now say "Brrrrr" with **Lip Trill** up and down the **Floors** in the shape of a **Pyramid** in an octave interval.

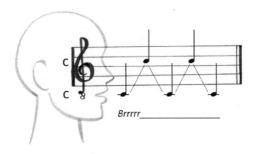

TWO-OCTAVE LIP TRILL EXERCISE

"Ssssss" with Lip Trill UP and DOWN 5ths

LET'S DO THIS!

This **Two-Octave Lip Trill Exercise** might very well be my favorite! If it's yours, great! If not, you can always substitute the Tongue Trill. Let's trill from middle C, going all the way up to high C, and back down again to middle C. Say "Ssssss" and then Lip Trill the five-note phrase going up by half steps. If high C feels too high for you, just go up to where it's comfortable and back down again. If you can go higher than high C, go for it!

GIVE IT A TRY!

- See your **Personalization** on your **Fourth Wall**

- Take an easy inhale – **The Breath**

- As you exhale with the **Support**, your bellybutton swings IN on **"Ssssss"**

- Now take a *new* **Breath** – then swing the bellybutton IN and slide the Lip Trill UP the five-note phrase

- As you slide UP the first five notes of the phrase, 1) bend your knees, and 2) at the same time, surrender your head *diving to the floor,* or flopping over like a rag doll, or nodding "yes" as you completely release the neck and upper torso – whichever feels more comfortable

- As you slide the Lip Trill back down the five-note phrase, stand straight UP and bring your head back up to see your person on the **Fourth Wall**

- As you go up half-step by half-step in the two-octave scale, guide the Lip Trill vibration up the **Floors** in the shape of a **Pyramid**

- As you climb higher and higher, *expect* the higher notes to become *smaller and smaller* living in the tight space of the **Attic** in the **Pyramid** – the image of the two balls will spin *faster and faster* with the lightning speed of **Tinker Bell** from your **Super Bellybutton Support** all the way up to high C

- Then, as you descend the **Floors** in the shape of the **Pyramid**, the belly-button continues to swing IN *leading* the tone, but the speed of the two balls spinning around each other slows down little by little as you make your way back to middle C

THE VOCAL EXERCISES ALL IN ONE PLACE

HAPPY BIRTHDAY – UP & DOWN 5ths EXERCISE

Sing the words *Happy Birthday* up and down 5ths from middle C all the way up two octaves to high C while *throwing the ball*. If high C feels too high for you, just go up to where it's comfortable and back down again. If you can go higher than high C, go for it!

SING THE HIGH NOTES "ON TOP"

As you jump up to the high 5th of each phrase, *think* of entering each high note singing **Bəth** of "Birthday" ON TOP. Throwing the ball *overhand* is a huge help to remind you of this instruction. But don't forget the lower notes too on the lower Floors of your Pyramid. No High Note Envy!

GIVE IT A TRY!

- Stand and see your partner or **Personalization** on your **Fourth Wall** while prepping the imaginary ball in your hand

- Keep seeing your person – feel your **Need** – and take an easy inhale – **The Breath**

- Initiate the **Support** from your Super Bellybutton swinging IN

- Feel the **Sensory Condition** of sunshine on your face and sing **Happy**

- Then throw the ball overhand to your person taking a big step forward with your front foot singing **B ə ə ə ə ə th** on the high 5th with the **Action** of "Hello! Greetings!" – feel the **Resonance** on the higher **Floor** in your Front Passage

- Keep throwing the ball as you finish down the 5th with **day**, as your person catches the ball

- If you have a partner, now they sing and throw the imaginary ball back to you and you catch the ball – keep going back and forth up the scale in half steps

- If you are alone, keep going up the scale throwing to your person on your **Fourth Wall** – keep singing half steps up the **Floors** of your Front Passage in the shape of the **Pyramid**

- Every time you throw the ball to the high 5th sing **Bəth** of "Birthday" ON TOP

- Be sure to come back DOWN the **Pyramid** for your lower notes on the lower **Floors** – No High Note Envy

WHAT ARE YOU AWARE OF?

How did it go? Is it fun practicing up and down the scale? These exercises together use all ten elements of *The Revolutionary Send*. **The Breath, Support, Resonance, Floors, Pyramid, Personalization, Fourth Wall, Sensory Condition, Need, and Action**. Using all of those elements at the same time takes practice. You got this!

THE VOCAL EXERCISES ALL IN ONE PLACE

EXTRA CREDIT: Keep going and try this new exercise!

HAPPY BIRTHDAY – UP & DOWN OCTAVES EXERCISE

Let's make the same exercise a bit more difficult. We worked on the octave leap in "Happy Birthday." Now sing *Happy Birthday* up and down the **octave** from middle C up to high G while *throwing the ball.* If high G feels easy, feel free to keep going!

SING THE HIGH NOTES "ON TOP"

As you jump up to the octave of each phrase, *think* of entering each high note singing *Bəth* of "Birthday" on a higher **Floor** ON TOP. Throwing the ball *overhand* is a huge help to remind you of this instruction. But don't forget the lower notes too on the lower **Floors** of your **Pyramid**. No High Note Envy!

GIVE IT A TRY!

- Stand and see your partner or **Personalization** on your **Fourth Wall** while prepping the imaginary ball in your hand

- Keep seeing your person – feel your **Need** – and take an easy inhale – **The Breath**

- Initiate the **Support** from your Super Bellybutton swinging IN

- Feel the **Sensory Condition** of sunshine on your face and sing **Happy**

- Then throw the ball *overhand* to your person taking a big step forward with your front foot singing **B ə ə ə ə ə th** on the octave leap with the **Action** of "Hello! Greetings!" – be aware you'll be jumping up to a higher **Floor** with the **Resonance** vibrating in a smaller space in the **Pyramid** as you add extra energy of your **Support**

- Keep throwing the ball as you finish down the octave with **day**, as your person catches the ball

- If you have a partner, now they sing and throw the imaginary ball back to you and you catch the ball – keep going back and forth up the scale in half steps

- If you are alone, keep going up the scale throwing to your person on your **Fourth Wall** – keep singing half steps up the **Floors** of your Front Passage in the shape of the **Pyramid**

- Every time you throw the ball up the octave, sing **Bəth** of "Birthday" on a much higher **Floor** entering ON TOP

- Be sure to come back DOWN the **Pyramid** for your lower notes on the lower **Floors** – No High Note Envy

WHAT ARE YOU AWARE OF?

How did it go doing your **Extra Credit**? Jumping up and down octaves is definitely a big leap! Did you jump from the lower to the higher **Floors** through the **Pyramid** increasing your **Super Bellybutton Support** with each leap? Throwing the ball to your **Personalization** on your **Fourth Wall** will help keep you to always SEND. You are using all ten elements of *The Revolutionary Send*. Bravo!

CONGRATULATIONS!

You Have Completed
THE VOCAL EXERCISES ALL IN ONE PLACE

I hope you're feeling proud of yourself! These vocal exercises may seem simple, but they are powerful tools that will serve you well.

chapter twelve

THE HEALING VOCAL EXERCISE

Before you start this exercise, take a little inventory. How do you feel? What are you aware of? Are you feeling stressed out? Does your voice feel tired? Is your body exhausted? Or maybe you're feeling good, and you'd like to wake up your voice? If you have pain in your throat from an illness, I suggest being on vocal rest and don't do the exercise. If the pain persists in your throat or you have any questions about your vocal health, it's always best to check with your doctor. Otherwise, please join me, and let's check in again after the exercise.

Here are the five sounds you'll be making during this exercise. Try them now:

"Ssssss" = like the sound of a snake

"Drrrrr" = Tongue Trill — like an Italian "R"

"Trrrrr" = *Unvoiced* Tongue Trill — just like a Tongue Trill but *without* your voice

"Brrrrr" = Lip Trill — like a kid making the sound of a motor boat

"Prrrrr" = *Unvoiced* Lip Trill — just like the Lip Trill, but *without* your voice

Find a comfy spot where you can sit, like a couch or an oversized recliner. Get super cozy with your head, neck, and shoulders *completely released* into the back of the couch or recliner with your feet resting on the floor or stretched out in front of you on an ottoman. Stay in this released position throughout the whole exercise.

As you begin each phrase, be sure to take an easy inhale, **The Breath** — then the bellybutton **Support** swinging IN on the exhale will *lead* every sound of the exercise for as long as you can go. (No judgment, just do what you can.) Notice that the bellybutton **Support** *swinging IN* is the *same* action as you do when you are standing. In fact, it might even feel easier! As long as you have your **Super Bellybutton Support** available, you can SING in *any* position. This exercise is proof!

Repeat each element three times as indicated.

"Sssss"

1. Inhale, and exhale on a long **"Sssss"**

   a. **Sssss**

   b. **Sssss**

   c. **Sssss**

2. Inhale, and as you exhale, crescendo and decrescendo on **"Sssss"** (slowly make it louder, then softer)

   a. **ssSSSSSSsss**

   b. **ssSSSSSSsss**

   c. **ssSSSSSSsss**

3. Inhale, and exhale pulsing the **"Sssss"** (louder/softer/louder/softer...)

   a. **ssssSSssSSssSSss**

   b. **ssSSssSSssSSssSSss**

   c. **ssSSssSSssSSssSSss**

UNVOICED TONGUE TRILL – "Trrrr"

1. Inhale, and exhale saying the *unvoiced* Tongue Trill **"Trrrr"**

   a. **Trrrr**

   b. **Trrrr**

   c. **Trrrr**

2. Inhale, and as you exhale, crescendo and decrescendo on **"Trrrr"** (slowly make it louder, then softer)

   a. **Trrrrrrrrrr**

   b. **Trrrrrrrrrr**

   c. **Trrrrrrrrrr**

3. Inhale, and exhale pulsing the *unvoiced* Tongue Trill **"Trrrrr"** (louder/softer/louder/softer...)

   a. **TrrRRrrRRrrRRrrRRrr**

   b. **TrrRRrrRRrrRRrrRRrr**

   c. **TrrRRrrRRrrRRrrRRrr**

4. Inhale, and exhale starting with the *unvoiced* Tongue Trill **"Trrrrr"** and then adding the *voice* **"Drrrrr"** – go back and forth between the two

   a. **TrrDrrTrrDrrTrrDrrTrrDrr**

   b. **TrrDrrTrrDrrTrrDrrTrrDrr**

   c. **TrrDrrTrrDrrTrrDrrTrrDrr**

TONGUE TRILL – "Drrrrr"

1. Inhale, and exhale saying the Tongue Trill **"Drrrrr"**

   a. **Drrrrr**

   b. **Drrrrr**

   c. **Drrrrr**

2. Inhale, and as you exhale, crescendo and decrescendo on **"Drrrrr"** (slowly make it louder, then softer)

   a. **Drrrrᴦᴦᴦᴦrrrr**

   b. **Drrrrᴦᴦᴦᴦrrrr**

   c. **Drrrrᴦᴦᴦᴦrrrr**

3. Inhale, and exhale pulsing the Tongue Trill **"Drrrrr"** (louder/softer/louder/softer...)

   a. **DrrRRrrRRrrRRrrRRrr**

   b. **DrrRRrrRRrrRRrrRRrr**

   c. **DrrRRrrRRrrRRrrRRrr**

4. Inhale, and sing these notes through the Tongue Trill **"Drrrrr"** three times:

Drrrrr_____

THE HEALING VOCAL EXERCISE

UNVOICED LIP TRILL – "Prrrrr"

1. Inhale, and exhale saying the *unvoiced* Lip Trill **"Prrrrr"**

   a. **Prrrrr**

   b. **Prrrrr**

   c. **Prrrrr**

2. Inhale, and as you exhale, crescendo and decrescendo on **"Prrrrr"** (slowly make it louder, then softer)

   a. **Prrrrｒｒｒrrrr**

   b. **Prrrrｒｒｒrrrr**

   c. **Prrrrｒｒｒrrrr**

3. Inhale, and exhale pulsing the *unvoiced* Lip Trill **"Prrrrr"** (louder/softer/louder/softer...)

   a. **PrrRRrrRRrrRRrrRRrr**

   b. **PrrRRrrRRrrRRrrRRrr**

   c. **PrrRRrrRRrrRRrrRRrr**

4. Inhale, and exhale starting with the *unvoiced* Lip Trill **"Prrrrr"** and then add the *voice* **"Brrrrr"** – go back and forth between the two

   a. **PrrBrrPrrBrrPrrBrrPrrBrr**

   b. **PrrBrrPrrBrrPrrBrrPrrBrr**

   c. **PrrBrrPrrBrrPrrBrrPrrBrr**

LIP TRILL – "Brrrrr"

1. Inhale, and exhale saying the Lip Trill **"Brrrrr"**

   a. **Brrrrr**

   b. **Brrrrr**

   c. **Brrrrr**

2. Inhale, and as you exhale, crescendo and decrescendo on **"Brrrrr"** (slowly make it louder, then softer)

   a. **Brrrrrrrrrrr**

   b. **Brrrrrrrrrrr**

   c. **Brrrrrrrrrrr**

3. Inhale, and exhale pulsing the Lip Trill **"Brrrrr"** (louder/softer/louder/softer...)

   a. **BrrRRrrRRrrRRrrRRrr**

   b. **BrrRRrrRRrrRRrrRRrr**

   c. **BrrRRrrRRrrRRrrRRrr**

4. Inhale, and sing these notes through the Lip Trill **"Brrrrr"** three times:

Brrrrr_____

WHAT ARE YOUR AWARE OF?

How do your body and voice feel now? Do they feel different than when you began? How is it different? Some of my students say afterwards their body feels like it's buzzing – they feel more relaxed – their voice feels calmer and comfortable. How about you? You can do this exercise several times a day if you like – just listen to your body. Be sure to stay hydrated.

epilogue

SINGING IS A MIRACLE

My Mom

At eighty-five-years-old my mother lived in a wonderful Senior Living community in Greenbrae, California with my stepfather. There was a health center there, and it was a beautiful place to live.

Mom's dementia had taken a turn for the worse that summer. We could converse and loved each other's company, but her words were mostly gibberish. Going out for lunch or a drive was tricky.

One sunny afternoon I decided to drive us just down the hill to our favorite haunt, Jamba Juice, and hoped that, if all went well, we could tack on a visit to my sister-in-law Beth's bakery in Mill Valley. It was a risk. The traffic was bad that day. Discomfort and fear could bring Mom misery when her brain switched to "worry channel" without warning or reason.

As we gathered ourselves into the car I let her know the situation. "Hey Mom, let's not venture too far...how about Jamba Juice? It would be fun to go see Beth and eat her delicious cookies — but it's a longer drive." Mom seemed happy with the plan, and we were off.

Northern California is so beautiful. I had lived there my whole life before heading east to follow my singing dream. That day was an extra special splendid one with bright sunshine and a gentle breeze. We sat outside sipping our yummy fruit smoothies through straws. I kept Mom engaged with lots of smiles and loving conversation. Maybe she wasn't all there, but she was my mom. She had always been my cheerleader for whatever I wanted to do in life. Now I was hers.

Mid-smoothie Mom looked up at me. As clear as a bell she said, "Let's go to Beth's." I hadn't heard a sentence from her in a long time that was so passionate and articulate – I didn't miss a beat. "Great, let's go!"

We jumped into the car, fastened seatbelts, and headed out. I swung onto 101 North. To my amazement, the bad traffic had magically cleared! Mom looked happy as a clam. I kept the joy going saying how fun it would be to see Beth! We parked behind the bakery with ease, just a few steps away from the front door.

As we entered the cute shop, every table was taken with one or two customers. The atmosphere was quiet – just a lazy hazy day of summer. Beth was joyous when we walked in. "You're here!" Mom and Beth adored each other.

After hugs and giggles, we ordered our cookies. I looked for a spot "for two" to sit. There was a guy softly playing the "bakery guitar" – the guitar that's left in the corner for anyone to pick up (like the "play me" pianos in airports). I asked if we could join him, and he waved us over.

"What song would you like to hear?"

"Well, we're both singers," I said.

"Is that right?" He didn't sound convinced. "Would you like to sing something?"

"Sure...do you know 'This Land is Your Land'?" (Mom and I loved singing this Woody Guthrie song together.)

"What key?"

"Any key." He smirked at my aplomb and launched into the intro.

I sang the first line, *This land is your land, this land is my land* – and his eyes popped out of his head as Mom joined in with PERFECT HARMONY! Every word was right! Her soaring soprano was stunning! And then, *everybody* in the bakery started singing! All the customers! All the workers! Beth ran over to us and was belting out every word hugging us! Suddenly, like a scene from a musical, the bakery door burst open revealing a long line of customers stretching onto the sidewalk. Everyone smiling and singing – *This land was made for you and me!*

As the song ended, everybody was laughing and simply on cloud nine. The guitar guy gushed, "So you ARE singers!" We thanked him, thanked Beth, and floated out the door, into the car, and sang song after song in perfect harmony all the way home.

It's one of the most glorious memories I'll have forever of my mother. Singing is a miracle.

Woody Guthrie wrote the uplifting anthem, "This Land is Your Land," as a tribute to those who had been displaced and suffered during the Great Depression of the 1930s.

ACKNOWLEDGEMENTS

I am in deep gratitude for so many who have helped me with this book.

First and foremost, my heartfelt thanks go to my beloved mentor and acting teacher of over thirty years, Susan Batson. Without you, my artistic career and my fulfilled happy life would not have come to fruition, let alone this book.

Thank you, Laura Moro of Curci Publishing in Milan, Italy, for being the first one who said "yes" to my book and to have brought me so much joy and friendship along the way.

Thank you to my literary agent, Susan Rabiner, for believing in my book and taking the long journey with me.

Thank you, Sierra Boggess. Your light has changed me. All my love and gratitude.

Thank you from the bottom of my heart Michael Bolton, Kerry Washington, Bella Thorne, James Gandolfini, John Turturro, Mary J. Blige, Tim Schōu, Simone, Kristen Blodgette, Eric Anthony Lopez, Jeff Bergman, Beth Setrakian, and all my students who have inspired me with your stories.

Thank you Buddy Kroll for bestowing upon me your brilliance and being an extraordinary lifelong friend.

Thank you Emilie Autumn for letting me into your exquisite creative world and gifting me with your knowledge through the lens of true friendship.

For helping me become a better writer, your keen eye, and for being a part of an incredible support team, thank you Jim Weitzer, Rob Miller, Terry Wollman, Kathe Mazur, Raffaele Passerini, Sibilla Buttiglione, Russell Arons, Vincent Vedrenne, Wendy Riese, and Luca Francesconi.

Thank you Chris Gunn for your wonderful illustrations. Eloïse Mueller, thank you for your technical support and perfection in every way. Thank you Derek Bishop for your gorgeous designs and friendship for over twenty years.

My voice and music teachers who changed my life, thank you Joan Heller, Phyllis Curtain, William Ramsey, Gary B. Walker, JD Nichols, Mark Pearson, Marie Gibson, and Corinne Swall.

All my gratitude to each and every teacher, student, friend, and colleague. The fact that our paths met is a gift I will always treasure.

Forever grateful to my father who knew my path and believed in me before I did, to my mother whose undying support and love still uplift me daily, and heartfelt gratitude to every member of my precious family. Special thanks to my beloved brothers – Scott, Rob, and Mark.

ABOUT THE AUTHOR...

Mary Setrakian is a native of San Francisco, California. She has been a resident of New York City for forty years performing professionally, in conjunction with teaching master voice to a variety of artists in New York, Los Angeles, and internationally in Italy, Australia, England, Portugal, Russia, and Armenia.

As a Master Voice Teacher, Mary prepared Nicole Kidman for her Golden Globe Award–winning and Oscar–nominated performance in Baz Luhrmann's *Moulin Rouge*. She has been the Master Voice Teacher to Oscar winners Forest Whitaker and Kate Winslet, Grammy award winners Michael Bolton and Mary J. Blige, as well as the stars of John Turturro's musical movie *Romance & Cigarettes*, including James Gandolfini, Mandy Moore, and Bobby Cannavale. Mary prepared Bella Thorne for her feature film singing debut in *Midnight Sun*. Mary was called upon by Disney to teach the leading players in the Broadway companies of Elton John's *Aida, Billy Elliot, The Lion King,* and Phil Collins' *Tarzan*. She was the vocal coach to Ben Daniels for his performance as Pontius Pilate in *JC Superstar Live on NBC* starring John Legend, and has been Broadway star Sierra Boggess' teacher since Sierra was 17 years old.

Mary has been seen on Broadway in *Hello, Dolly!* starring Carol Channing. She toured with the Broadway companies of *The Phantom of the Opera* (Madame Giry), *Les Miserables, Hello, Dolly!,* and the World Tour of *Evita* (as Eva Peron in Duisburg, Germany). Mary was featured at Carnegie Hall in *Jubilee* directed by Herbert Ross.

Mary's award winning "Best Actress" regional roles include Fanny Brice in *Funny Girl*, Trina in *Falsettos*, the Narrator in *Joseph and the Amazing Technicolor Dreamcoat*, and her critically acclaimed one-woman show, *A New York Romance*. The LA Times exclaimed "Chanteuse Setrakian is ... dazzling!"

Mary holds a Masters in Voice Performance with Distinction from the New England Conservatory and is a graduate of Stanford University in Music/Voice with Honors. She studied at the Tanglewood Music Festival with Phyllis Curtain and was a voice student of Joan Heller, Mark Pearson, Marie Gibson, and Corinne Swall. She has studied acting with her mentor, Susan Batson, for over thirty years.

INDEX